COHESION IN LITERARY TEXTS

A Study of Some Grammatical and Lexical Features

of English Discourse

by

WALDEMAR GUTWINSKI

Glendon College, York University

1976

MOUTON

THE HAGUE · PARIS

ISBN 90 279 3413 4

COPYRIGHT ACKNOWLEDGEMENTS

PREFACE

In this book I attempt a cautious step into the unexplored terrain which lies between literary and linguistic studies. I propose a linguistic framework for the study of cohesion in literary texts, apply it to passages from Ernest Hemingway and Henry James, and point out certain implications for the now rapidly developing studies in discourse structure and literary stylistics.

The book is a revision and enlargement of my doctoral dissertation submitted to the Graduate Faculty of the University of Connecticut in the spring of 1969. Chapter 1 is completely rewritten to account for developments in discourse studies relevant to cohesion. A glance at section 1.1. will indicate that most of the works mentioned have appeared since the original study was completed. In a book of this size it has not been possible to account for all studies relating to textual analysis, such as work presently under way in continental Europe. Also, because this study confines itself to written literary texts, except for one reference to Labov's work on narratives, no account is given of the burgeoning area of research into discourse by anthropologists and sociolinguists.

I would like to acknowledge my debt to Professors Margaret Schlauch and Alfred Reszkiewicz who, while I was a student at Warsaw University, instilled in me a lasting interest in the English language and scholarship. While writing the original dissertation I had the benefit of discussions with and encouragement from Kenneth G. Wilson, Milton R. Stern, and Thomas J. Roberts. I am much indebted to H. A. Gleason, Jr. for his continued guidance and stimulation both during the writing of the dissertation and the preparation of the book. Special thanks go to Grace Jolly who read the manuscript at several stages and provided helpful comments. I have also benefited from discussions about linguistics and literature with several other of my colleagues in Glendon's innovative English Department. Finally I must thank Jeffrey Zahn, most competent of research assistants and Mary Lisabeth Golding who prepared the index.

The initial research for this study was supported by predoctoral fellowships from the University of Connecticut. Two York University minor research grants assisted in the subsequent work.

Glendon College, York University   Waldemar F. Gutwinski
Toronto, Canada
July, 1973

TABLE OF CONTENTS

LIST OF FIGURES AND TABLES

Figure

Table

INTRODUCTION

1.1. PRESENT STATE OF DISCOURSE STUDIES

The structure of connected discourse is currently receiving growing attention from various linguists, especially those following the tagmemic and stratificational models of language. It is considered one of the topics of primary importance at the frontiers of current linguistic theory and is connected closely with at least one other important area of linguistic research today, semantic structure and its relation to syntax.

Until relatively recently the sentence was generally considered the upper limit of linguistic investigation. But as Harris noted in 1951, the reasons for not attempting to study the interrelations among whole utterances within discourse were pragmatic rather than theoretical.[1] More recently several linguists have approached the problem of linguistic structure beyond the sentence. Studies of the structure of parts of texts and even of whole texts began appearing in the late fifties and early sixties.[2] Some such studies were by Loriot,[3] Gudschinsky,[4] Pickett,[5] Loos,[6] and Powlison.[7] Sarah

---

[1] Zellig Harris, *Methods in Structural Linguistics* (Chicago, 1951), 11-12.

[2] Hockett's work on Potawatomi syntax is an isolated early attempt at discourse analysis. Charles Hockett, "Potawatomi Syntax", *Language* 15, 235-248.

[3] James Loriot, "Shipibo Discourse Analysis", *The Bible Translator* (New York, July 1957). See also James Loriot and Barbara Hollenbach, "Shipibo Paragraph Structure", *Foundations of Language* 6, 43-66.

[4] Sarah Gudschinsky, "Discourse Analysis of a Mazatec Text", *International Journal of American Linguistics* 15, 139-146.

Gudschinsky, for example, used techniques elaborated by Harris,[8] which consist of assigning words and phrases to "equivalence classes" based on their occurrence in identical or equivalent environments and of applying certain transformations. Gudschinsky applied these techniques in her analysis of a text in Mazatec, an Amerindian language of Southern Mexico. Kenneth Pike[9] and others developed a tagmemic framework for discourse analysis which has been applied in discourse studies dealing mostly with texts in non-Indo-European languages.

In the later sixties and the early seventies we observe an increased interest in the study of discourse structure. While the number of discourse studies in non-Indo-European languages using the tagmemic framework have increased (e.g. Longacre,[10] Reid,[11]

---

[5]   Velma Pickett, *The Grammatical Hierarchy of Isthmus Zapotec* (Baltimore, 1960).

[6]   Eugene Loos, "Copanahua Narrative Structure", *University of Texas Studies in Literature and Linguistics* 4, 699-742.

[7]   Paul Powlison, "A Paragraph Analysis of a Yagua Folktale", *International Journal of American Linguistics* 31, 109-118.

[8]   Zellig Harris, "Discourse Analysis" and "Discourse Analysis: A Sample Text", *Language* 28, 1-30 and 474-494. For more information on Harris' method of discourse analysis and exemplification of his analysis of a technical article in English, see Zellig Harris, *Transformations and Discourse Analysis Papers*, reissued in *Discourse Analysis Reprints* (The Hague, 1963).

[9]   Kenneth Pike, "Discourse Analysis of Tagmemic Matrices", *Oceanic Linguistics* 3, 5-25. See also Kenneth Pike, "Beyond the Sentence", *College Composition and Communication* 15, 129-135, and Kenneth Pike, *Language in Relation to a Unified Theory of the Structure of Human Behavior* (The Hague, 1967), 424-431, 484-486, and, in regard to Pike's conception of the interlocking of the lexical and grammatical hierarchies, pp. 573-574.

[10]   Robert Longacre, *Discourse, Paragraph, and Sentence Structure in Selected Philippine Languages*, Volumes I, II, III (Santa Ana, Calif., 1968). In the introduction to Volume I, using some Turkish data as illustration, Longacre gives a brief orientation to the concepts and terminology of tagmemics, a useful source of such information for those wishing to follow tagmemic discussions of discourse structure. Cf. Longacre, *Discourse, Paragraph and Sentence Structure*, pp. i-xxi. See also Part 1 of Volume I for a detailed exposition of Longacre's theory of discourse structure and heuristic (the "seven articles of faith", as Longacre refers to them informally) and a discussion of frequently occurring discourse genre: narrative, procedural, expository, and hortatory (pp. 1-40).

[11]   Lawrence Reid, *Central Bontoc: Sentence, Pargaraph and Discourse*

Wise[12]), studies dealing with various aspects of English discourse (e.g. Williams,[13] Kittredge,[14] Klammer[15]) have begun to appear.

Also on the increase is the number of discourse studies using more or less eclectic approaches. Among these we may mention Longacre's final two-volume report containing a discussion of the analysis of sentence, paragraph, and discourse in several New Guinea languages (Volume I), together with the analyzed texts (Volume II).[16] Chapter 3 of Volume I, which is entitled "A Taxonomy of the Deep Structure of Propositions",[17] follows from an earlier work of Ballard, Conrad, and Longacre[18] and is "based on an expansion and refinement of the Statement Calculus of formal logic".[19] This chapter reflects a certain degree of convergence

---

(Norman, Oklahoma, 1970). Reid, who like Longacre is a worker for SIL and a practitioner of tagmemics, uses Longacre's *Discourse, Paragraph and Sentence Structure* for his theoretical framework.

[12] Mary Ruth Wise, "Identification of Participants in Discourse: A Study of Aspects of Form and Meaning in Nomatsiguenga", unpublished doctoral dissertation (University of Michigan, 1968).

[13] Joseph Marek Williams,"Some Grammatical Characteristics of Continuous Discourse", unpublished doctoral dissertation (University of Wisconsin, 1966) deals with two groups of grammatical linking devices which function in interclausal and intersentential relations in English.

[14] Richard Kittredge, "Tense, Aspect, and Conjunction: Some Inter-Relations for English", unpublished doctoral dissertation (University of Pennsylvania, 1969). Kittredge makes use of a system of transformational operators developed by Zellig Harris in *Mathematical Structures of Language* (New York, 1968).

[15] Thomas Klammer, "The Structure of Dialogue Paragraphs in Written English Dramatic and Narrative Discourse", unpublished doctoral dissertation (University of Michigan, 1971). The approach is tagmemic.

[16] Robert Longacre, *Hierarchy and Universality of Discourse Constituents in New Guinea Languages*, Volumes I and II (Washington, D.C., 1972).

[17] Longacre, *Hierarchy and Universality of Discourse*, 51-92. Several English illustrations are given in this chapter which should be of general interest from the point of view of the theory and heuristic procedures of discourse analysis.

[18] D. Lee Ballard, Robert J. Conrad, and Robert E. Longacre, "The Deep and Surface Grammar of Interclausal Relations", *Foundations of Language* 7, 70-118.

[19] Longacre, *Hierarchy and Universality of Discourse*, 51. There is a parallel between Longacre's taxonomy of the "deep structure interclausal relations" and Fillmore's ("The Case for Case", *Universals of Linguistic Theory*, ed. by Emmon Bach and Robert T. Harms (New York, 1968), 1-88) "cases". See Longacre, *Hierarchy and Universality of Discourse*, pp. 52ff.

of tagmemics with some features of generative transformationalism (especially with the 'case' grammar and generative semantics).[20] In Chapter (4) of Longacre's book an interpretation of some surface structures in three New Guinea languages is given in the light of the deep structure relations.

A study of discourse forms in Saramaccan by Grimes and Glock[21] is perhaps the best example of an eclectic approach to discourse analysis when we consider that the authors apply the notion of semantic deep structure which is dependent on, among others, Fillmore's case grammar,[22] Halliday's systemic grammar,[23] and Gleason's stratificational statement of semologic structure for narratives.[24] Bromley's study of discourse features of a non-Austronesian language in Indonesia,[25] although it is informed by a stratificational model, is also eclectic in its approach.

Particularly promising are the discourse studies by Gleason's students at the Hartford Seminary Foundation which follow a stratificational model. They are, in the order of appearance, Charles Taber's work on Sango narrative, with its description of the stratificational model (compared with transformation-generative, tagmemic, and scale-and-category grammars) and its treatment

[20] See also Robert E. Longacre, "Sentence Structure as a Statement Calculus", *Language* 46, 783-815.
[21] Joseph Grimes and Naomi Glock, "A Saramaccan Narrative Pattern", *Language* 46, 408-425.
[22] Charles Fillmore, "The Case for Case". See also Charles Fillmore, "The Grammar of *Hitting* and *Breaking*", *Readings in English Transformational Grammar*, ed. by R. A. Jacobs and P. S. Rosenbaum (Waltham, Mass., 1970), 120-133.
[23] M. A. K. Halliday, "Notes on Transitivity and Theme in English", *Journal of Linguistics* 3, 37-81, 199-244. Cf. also M. A. K. Halliday, "Options and Functions in the English Clause", *Brno Studies in English* 8, 81-88; M. A. K. Halliday, "Language Structure and Language Function", *New Horizons in Linguistics*, ed. by John Lyons (Harmondsworth: Penguin Books), 140-165; M. A. K. Halliday, "Functional Diversity in Language as Seen from a Consideration of Modality and Mood in English", *Foundations of Language* 6, 322-361.
[24] H. A. Gleason, Jr., "Contrastive Analysis in Discourse Structure", *Monograph Series on Languages and Linguistics* 21, ed. by James E. Alatis (Washington, D.C., 1968), 39-63.
[25] H. Myron Bromley, "The Grammar of Lower Grand Valley Dani in Discourse Perspective", unpublished doctoral dissertation (Yale University, 1972).

of the sememic and lexemic strata;[26] Robert Cromack's discussion of "core" and "cohesion" systems in discourse structure in Cashinawa (an Amerindian language in Peru);[27] Leslie Stennes' study of the identification of participants in Fulani (a language in West Africa) as one element of discourse structure;[28] and Grace Jolly's study of poetic discourse in Nyisi (a Tibeto-Burman language in Northeast India), with its discussion of generic constraints, especially those operating on the grammatic stratum.[29]

Gleason's own published work is a programmatic statement of the nature of discourse structure studies following a stratificational model, with emphasis on the semologic structure of narratives.[30] The latter will be discussed in section 2.3.1. in relation to our study of cohesion.

While one notes a growing interest in 'discourse grammar'[31] on the part of linguists using a transformational-generative framework, there are, so far, no major studies available in print. This is probably due to the fact that transformational-generative grammarians originally set as their goal formulation of rules for generation of individual sentences only. According to Langendoen (in *The Essentials of English Grammar*), that was a conscious choice on the part of some grammarians who restricted their attention to formulating "the rules that are necessary for the explicit construction of sentences of a language, omitting the problem of formulating the rules for constructing larger linguistic entities, such as paragraphs or discourses", as well as omitting the problem of the use

---

[26] Charles R. Taber, *The Structure of Sango Narrative* (Hartford, Conn., 1966).
[27] Robert E. Cromack, *Language Systems and Discourse Structure in Cashinawa* (Hartford, Conn., 1968).
[28] Leslie H. Stennes, *The Identification of Participants in Adamawa Fulani* (Hartford, Conn., 1969).
[29] Grace Jolly, "Nyisi Poetic Devices", unpublished doctoral dissertation (Hartford Seminary Foundation, 1970).
[30] Gleason, "Contrastive Analysis in Discourse Structure".
[31] Often contrasted with 'sentence grammar'. See, for example, Robert Stockwell, Paul Schachter, and Barbara Hall Partee, *The Major Syntactic Structures of English* (New York, 1973).

of language in situations.[32] But for most transformational gener-
ativists the limitation to sentence grammar followed from a conviction that the sentence was the largest linguistic unit.

Wolfgang Dressler's article[33] is an example of a growing dis-
satisfaction with the restriction of transformational work to sentence grammar and treating such discourse phenomena as "anaphora or substitution or cross-reference or, more restricted, coref-
erence" by means of extending the rules of setence grammar as
well as camouflaging certain discourse regularities under such notions as presuppositions.[34] A more recent example of a change in
attitude towards discourse structure studies on the part of linguists following a transformational model is Charles Ruhl's
article in the April, 1973 issue of *Language Sciences* in which he
proposes to "consider, in the context of Transformational Grammar, the rhetorical notion of *coherence*: how it can be defined, how
it can be incorporated into transformational theory, and what
consequences it holds for that theory".[35] It is interesting to note
that the article takes into account contributions of other schools of

<hr/>

[32]   D. Terence Langendoen, *Essentials of English Grammar* (New York, 1970),
3-4. Langendoen says that the reason for this situation in what he calls "most
grammatical discussions", his own (in *Essentials*) included, "is simply that the
obstacles confronting anyone who even wants to make a start at tackling the
latter two problems, i.e., discourse structure and the use of sentences in situa-
tional context are so disproportionately immense at present that it is usually
not thought to be worth the effort" (p. 4). In this study, needless to say, we do
not share Langendoen's appreciation of the situation in present-day linguistics
(or of that in the sixties).

[33]   Wolfgang Dressler, "Towards a Semantic Deep Structure of Discourse
Grammar", *Papers from the Sixth Regional Meeting of the Chicago Linguistic
Society* (Chicago, 1970).

[34]   Dressler, "Towards a Semantic Deep Structure of Discourse Grammar",
202. See also W. Ross Winterowd, "The Grammar of Coherence", *College
English* 31, 828-835. Winterowd begins his argument for a grammar of "coherence" by observing that transformational generative grammar fails "just at
the point where it could best serve rhetoric", i.e. it does not go beyond the
sentence boundary. Winterowd then goes on to say, "The significance of this
limitation is underscored by the inability of grammarians to write a rule for the
simplest of all transformations: clause coordination" (Winterowd, "The
Grammar of Coherence", 828).

[35]   Charles Ruhl, "Prerequisites for a Linguistic Description of Coherence",
Language Sciences 25, 15-18

linguistics, for example those by the Prague School linguists and Halliday under the term "functional sentence perspective"[36] which concern certain communication factors and which "have been virtually ignored in generative grammar".[37]

Although not dealing directly or exclusively with the problems of discourse structure, M.A.K. Halliday's work has some important implications for discourse analysis. The original statement of cohesion,[38] the distinction of "given" and "new" in the clause considered as a unit of the organization of information in English, the development of the Prague School's concept of theme and rheme, the formulation of transitivity functions (such as process and participant roles) and their relation to elements of clause structure, the distinction of the "textual" function of language and the statement of its relationship to two other functions ("ideational" and "interpersonal") are some of Halliday's contributions[39] to modern linguistic theory and description which have much relevance for formulating statements about the nature of the structure of connected discourse. Halliday's statement of cohesion was, for example, a starting point for the present study.

In recent years, then, one observes a developing awareness of grammatical relations which obtain across sentence boundaries as well as an ever-increasing interest in discourse structure in general.

[36] Cf. Halliday, "Functional Diversity in Language".

[37] Ruhl, "Prerequisites for a Linguistic Description of Coherence", 17-18. We may note that in this new climate linguistic studies begin to appear of texts which deal with relations that cross sentence boundaries and which avail themselves, to greater or lesser degree, of the transformational apparatus, e.g. Carl H. Harrison, "Syntactical Aspects of Asurini Monologue Discourse", unpublished doctoral dissertation (University of Pennsylvania, 1970) and Carlota S. Smith, "Sentences in Discourse: An Analysis of a Discourse by Bertrand Russell", *Journal of Linguistics* 7, 213-235.

[38] M. A. K. Halliday, "Descriptive Linguistics in Literary Studies", *English Studies Today*, ed. by G. I. Duthie (Edinburgh, 1964), 25-39, and M. A. K. Hallidav, "The Linguistic Study of Literary Texts", *Proceedings of the Ninth International Congress of Linguists*, ed. by Horace G. Lunt (The Hague, 1964), 302-307.

[39] Cf. Halliday, "Transitivity and Theme"; "Options and Functions"; "Language Structure and Language Function"; and "Functional Diversity in Language".

One need only note that the most comprehensive grammar of contemporary English, published in 1972 by Randolph Quirk, Sidney Greenbaum, Geoffrey Leech, and Jan Svartvik, devotes an entire chapter to "Sentence Connection", also noting in other chapters the problem of discourse reference.[40] Currently in preparation by M.A.K. Halliday and Ruqaiya Hasan is a book devoted entirely to English discourse structure under the heading of COHESION.[41]

While a systematic interest in the problems of structure in discourse on the part of linguists has appeared only recently, these problems have been discussed from various grounds by literary critics and by the teachers of composition and rhetoric. But such discussions, although some are linguistically insightful, lack a sufficiently comprehensive and rigorous descriptive apparatus to qualify as descriptions of the structure of English. The topics studied include such varied concepts as theme, plot, diction, punctuation, plan, style, unity, figures of speech, paragraphs, chapters, leitmotiv, and use of pronouns, sequence of tenses, lexical substitutes, coherence, reference, and coordination and subordination. These discussions have prepared the ground for more rigorous, if somewhat less inclusive, linguistic investigations of literary texts in respect to the structure of units larger than sentences. It appears logical that a good place to begin the study of discourse in English will be with written literary texts which have already received much critical analysis touching at various points on the concerns of the lin-

[40] Randolph Quirk, Sidney Greenbaum, Geoffrey Leech, and Jan Svartvik, *A Grammar of Contemporary English* (London, 1972), 649-716. One might note that, although not directly addressed to sentence connection, the recently published grammar by Stockwell, Schachter, and Partee has one chapter on "Conjunction" containing a discussion of certain relations which in this study would be designated as relating to discourse structure.

[41] M. A. K. Halliday and Ruqaiya Hasan, "Cohesion in Modern English" (Longmans English Language Series, London, forthcoming). Given the usefulness of Halliday's original statement on cohesion (cf. Halliday, "The Linguistic Study of Literary Texts") and of Hasan's already published work on grammatical cohesion (Ruqaiya Hasan, *Grammatical Cohesion in Spoken and Written English: Part One* (London, Longmans, 1968), the forthcoming book promises to be a significant contribution to our understanding of discourse structure in English.

guistic study of English discourse. Hence the choice of passages by Hemingway and James for examination in this study.

1.2. THEORETICAL MODEL

There are at present several competing theories of language organization, the most important of which are: the extended standard theory of generative transformational grammar (Chomsky et al); generative semantics (Lakoff, McCawley); applicational-generative (Šaumjan et al in the U.S.S.R.); tagmemic (Pike and the Wycliffe Bible Translators); systemic, also known as 'scale-and-category' (Halliday); and stratificational (Gleason, Lamb).

Like linguists operating with the assumptions of the stratificational model, those using the tagmemic and the systemic models recognize the requirement that linguistic analysis be applicable to whole texts. They have made a number of insightful contributions to the field of discourse analysis. Those using the tagmemic model often have a wide experience with world languages. Their strong data orientation forces them to recognize and attack the problems of connected discourse. A number of the studies referred to in this chapter are made within the tagmemic framework.

Those linguists who use the systemic grammar have frequently given their attention to written and literary texts. The indebtedness of this study to Halliday will be apparent throughout. However, at the time this study was undertaken neither the tagmemic nor the scale-and-category theory had developed a semology or even a fully worked-out tactics for its upper stratum (lexical hierarchy or lexis). This must be seen as an inadequacy if any explicitness is attempted.

Linguists developing the transformational-generative theory have concerned themselves less with connected discourse than have the other groups. However, they have recognized the place of the semantic component. Until recently the insistence that the sentence is the largest unit of discourse disqualified the transformational-generative theory from serving as a model for discourse structure.

It is true that Katz and Fodor[42] recognized that a semantic theory needs to provide for disambiguation of sequences of sentences as well as of individual sentences and that it needs to take into account "setting in a discourse", that is, other sentences which are in some relation to those under consideration. But, while recognizing the problem, they suggested what seems a very unsatisfactory solution, the treatment of a text as a single sentence by treating sentence boundaries as connectives. It seems that renaming a text a sentence has changed nothing, while the assumption that the "and-conjunction" is a simple matter is unwarranted, *and* being the least marked of connectors.

Since this study was completed, well-marked trends have appeared from within the generative-transformational movement. Extended standard theory seems to continue the older transformational generative attitudes towards discourse. Generative semantics has been giving a great deal of attention to presuppositions, including under this rubric various contextual matters, thus opening a line of investigation of discourse structure. Various other minor developments from transformational generativism, mostly unnamed, have taken place and linguists following these have begun to be interested in discourse structure and are attacking the problems in various ways.

Though one of the other theories may be preferable to another, none of them seems adequate for adoption as a theoretical model in this study. None has a sufficiently developed semology. A model of semologic structure has to underlie any serious attempt to handle connected discourse. Stratificational theory has been adopted as the theoretical framework here because it recognizes and develops several strata, one of which is semology.

The statement of the problem of discourse structure and the direction in which the analysis will proceed depends to a great extent on which view of language organization we adopt. In the present investigation the stratificational model of language organization as

---

[42] Jerrold J. Katz and Jerry Fodor, "The Structure of a Semantic Theory", *Language* 39, 170-210.

developed by Gleason and Lamb provides the theoretical basis. A general description of the model with a stress on those parts which have a particular relevance for discourse structure will be given in Chapter 2. At the moment it will suffice to say that according to the stratificational theory there are three major components, called strata, of language.[43] They are phonology, grammar, and semology. The linguistic phenomena studied here belong to the grammatic stratum. Reference will be made to the semologic stratum as well.

1.3. PLACE OF DISCOURSE STRUCTURE IN THE STRATIFICATIONAL MODEL

A truly comprehensive description of the discourse structure of a text can be made only by stating it in terms of the units of, and the relations obtaining on, the semologic stratum. At present too little is known about these units and relations in English to allow a full discourse analysis of an English text. The structure of the semologic stratum is not directly observable since it is not represented directly in the grammar and even less so in the phonology of the language. But this deeper, underlying structure finds its manifestation in the relatively shallower structure of the grammar and is still recoverable from it.

1.4. COHESION AS A LINGUISTIC CONCEPT ALLOWING THE STUDY OF DISCOURSE FEATURES ON THE GRAMMATIC STRATUM

A fruitful avenue for English discourse studies lies, then, in the examination of these units and relations obtaining on the grammatic stratum which are felt to be realizations of the discourse structure on the semologic stratum. The present study takes this ap-

---

[43] Sidney Lamb, *Outline of Stratificational Grammar* (Washington, D.C., 1966), 1.

proach by examining the cohesive relations obtaining between clauses and sentences of some selected literary prose texts.

1.4.1. Definition of cohesion

The term COHESION is used in this investigation for the relations obtaining among the sentences and clauses of a text. These relations, which occur on the grammatic stratum, are signalled by certain grammatical and lexical features reflecting discourse structure on a higher, semologic stratum. These features, such as anaphora, subordination, and coordination, are called COHESIVE. They account for what may also be referred to as the textual connectivity of sentences and clauses. They do not by themselves constitute cohesion but they mark which clauses and setences are related and in what manner. This relatedness of clauses and sentences constitutes the internal cohesion of a text. Cohesion as defined in this study does not constitute discourse structure but it reflects indirectly, perhaps in part only, the underlying semologic structure of a text, that is, the discourse structure conceived at the semologic stratum.

1.4.2. Cohesion and 'coherence'

The terms COHESION, COHESIVE, and COHESIVENESS as used in this study, should not be confused with the terms 'coherence', 'coherency', and 'coherent', frequently used in textbooks of rhetoric and composition, although some grammatical devices usually mentioned in the discussions of 'coherence' will be studied in this investigation under the heading of cohesion. The rhetoric textbooks define 'coherence' rather vaguely, dealing under that heading with phenomena which, from a linguistic point of view, cannot be treated on a single level of analysis and some of which are not open to linguistic investigation at all. 'Coherence' is most often discussed in relation to the paragraph. A well constructed paragraph is said to be characterized by 'unity' and 'coherence'. 'Unity' is achieved when all sentences in the paragraph "relate to a single point represented by a topic sentence". 'Coherence' is achieved when the sentences "follow each other in a logical order and are linked together by *transitions*".[44] Another definition of 'coherence' runs as follows:

Literally, the word *cohere* means to hold together. A paragraph is said to have coherence when its sentences are woven together or flow into each other. If a paragraph is coherent, the reader moves easily from one sentence to the next without feeling that there are gaps in the thought, puzzling jumps, or points not made.[45]

McCrimmon then goes on to say that a paragraph is more coherent when the author has provided transitions between thoughts expressed in its sentences. He tells his readers that these transitions are created by two means: "sometimes by filling a small gap in the thought, thus providing better continuity of statement, sometimes by connecting words and phrases which tie sentences together".[46]

It is apparent from the above citations that the term 'coherence', inasmuch as it refers to linguistic features of a text, is used indiscriminately and in a vague manner to cover phenomena which ought to be studied on at least two levels. Such things as "gaps in thought" are not open to linguistic investigation. Characteristics of the paragraph like the order of the presentation and the continuity of statement could probably be dealt with on the semologic stratum. Transitions between sentences, inasmuch as they are discussed in terms of grammatical categories such as conjunctions and pronouns, should be dealt with separately as markers signalling on the grammatic stratum the structure of the paragraph that was conceived on the semologic stratum.

Because of the vagueness that accompanies the popular use of the term 'coherence', and the indiscriminate application of it to a wide range of linguistic and non-linguistic phenomena, this term is carefully avoided in this study. The term COHESION, introduced by

---

[44] William Watt, *An American Rhetoric* (New York, 1959), 54.
[45] James McCrimmon, *Writing with a Purpose*, 4th ed. (Boston, 1967), 120. For a more recent discussion of 'coherence', attempting to develop a generative rhetoric, see Winterowd, "The Grammar of Coherence".
[46] McCrimmon, *Writing with a Purpose*, 122.

Halliday explicitly for the purpose of linguistic analysis, is used instead in the sense which was defined earlier.

1.4.3. Halliday's statement of cohesion

The concept of cohesion developed in this study is primarily dependent on M.A.K. Halliday who originally stated it in a different context.[47] In Halliday's "The Linguistic Study of Literary Texts", the concept of cohesion allows the gathering together of various lexical and grammatical categories which can be useful in the linguistic study of literary texts. He does not define cohesion beyond stating that it is "a syntagmatic relation and, insofar as it is grammatical, it is partly accounted for by structure".[48] Halliday then adds some explanatory statements which make his exposition of interest for the purposes of discourse studies:

Structure, however, is not the only cohesive factor operating at the level of grammar. There are certain grammatical categories whose exponents cohere with other items in the text, items to which they do not stand in a fixed structural relation or indeed necessarily in any structural relation at all. Principal among these are the anaphoric items in the nominal and adverbial group: deictics, submodifiers and adverbs, of which the most frequent are "the", "this", "that", the personal possessives, "such", "so", "there" and "then"; and the (personal) pronouns... Lexical cohesion in its clearest form is carried by two or more occurrences, in close proximity, of the same lexical item, or of items paradigmatically related in the sense that they may belong to the same lexical set. For example, in a passage by Leslie Stephen one paragraph ends "I took leave, and turned to the ascent of the peak"; the next paragraph begins "The climb is perfectly easy". Thus in the new paragraph the first lexical item, "climb", coheres with "ascent"; later occur "mountain" and "summit" cohering with "peak".[49]

---

[47]   M. A. K. Halliday, "The Linguistic Study of Literary Texts". The paper was originally given in 1962. See also M. A. K. Halliday, "Descriptive Linguistics in Literary Studies", in *Patterns of Language*, by Angus McIntosh and M. A. K. Halliday (London, 1966), 56-59, for a brief discussion of cohesion in three short excerpts from literary texts.

[48]   The term "structure" is used here in a restricted sense.

[49]   Halliday, "The Linguistic Study of Literary Texts", 304.

Halliday gives the following listing of the categories subsumed under the heading of cohesion:

A. Grammatical
   1. Structural (clauses in sentence structure)
      (a) Dependence
      (b) Linking
   2. Non-structural
      (a) Anaphora
         (i) deictics and submodifiers
         (ii) pronouns
      (b) Substitution
         (i) verbal
         (ii) nominal
B. Lexical
   1. Repetition of item
   2. Occurrence of item from same lexical set[50]

The importance for the present study of Halliday's work on what he named "cohesion" lies in the fact that he observed, brought together, and classified, although without saying so, a number of the phenomena which constitute some of the grammatic features of discourse. "Grammatic" is used here as a term covering the phenomena on the grammatic stratum of the language as opposed to those on the semologic and phonologic strata. Halliday has to be credited, therefore, with bringing together and classifying a number of linguistic phenomena that will be studied in this book. But he did not account for them, as the present study seeks to do, by placing them in the framework of discourse structure, the concept of which is informed by the stratificational theory. Consequently, Halliday's cohesive categories can be seen as features which represent on the grammatic (morphemic and lexemic) stratum, some of the manifestations of the discourse structure from the semologic stratum.

[50] Halliday, "The Linguistic Study of Literary Texts", 303.

1.4.4. Hasan's study of cohesion

Ruqaiya Hasan's contribution to studies on cohesion dates back to her University of Edinburgh doctoral thesis of 1964.[51] Following Halliday's statement, she lists under the heading of cohesion some of the linguistic features of the style of two contemporary English prose writers. Most of these features belong to what Halliday calls structural cohesion. Hasan uses for the latter kind of cohesion the term "major cohesion" while her term "minor cohesion" would cover cohesive features which Halliday groups under lexical cohesion.

In a subsequent work, entitled *Grammatical Cohesion in Spoken and Written English: Part One*, Hasan distinguishes between the internal and the external features characterizing a text ("what makes a text hang together") and points out that it is only the internal (linguistic) features of "textuality" which are referred to under the name of cohesion. She restricts the use of the term cohesion to inter-sentence relations.[52] Hasan's *Grammatical Cohesion* is an amply illustrated account of cohesive features which she places under the rubrics of "reference" and "substitution" and which in the present study are subsumed under the heading of -phoric relations (with only anaphora and cataphora functioning cohesively).

In a later article called "Rime and Reason in Literature"[53] Ruqaiya Hasan adds to "reference" and "substitution", "ellipsis" and "logical connectives", to give four "general grammatical cohesive tie-types" and deals also with some aspects of lexical organization relevant to cohesion. The whole is placed in the context of its implications for literary style.[54]

---

[51] Ruqaiya Hasan, "A Linguistic Study of Contrastive Features in the Style of Two Contemporary English Prose Writers", unpublished doctoral thesis (University of Edinburgh, 1964).
[52] Hasan, *Grammatical Cohesion*, 1-9, 18-19.
[53] Ruqaiya Hasan, "Rime and Reason in Literature", *Literary Style: A Symposium*, ed. by Seymour Chatman (New York, 1971), 299-326.
[54] Hasan is currently working on a volume called "Language in the Imaginative Context: A Sociolinguistic Study of Stories Told by Children" (to be pub-

1.4.5. Other work relating to cohesion

The most recent work on cohesion is Crowell's "Cohesion in Bororo Discourse" (1973)[55] where tagmemic and systemic insights are brought to bear very effectively on Bororo text. Cohesion is viewed as a means of providing among other things temporal, spatial, and logical orientation for the hearer.

Using an early transformational-generative framework Ohmann[56] has examined short excerpts from Hemingway, Faulkner, James, and Lawrence. By means of what Nida would call "back transformation" or "decomposition"[57] Ohmann rewrites the excerpts and compares them with the author's original texts, describing alternative styles in terms of employment of different sets of transformations. What is being compared falls under the heading of style because two different surface structures are being compared. However no satisfactory account of deep structure is given and consequently it is difficult to see what relationships would obtain between the deep and surface structures of these texts.[58]

Using the categories of scholarly traditional grammar and rhetoric, Moss[59] has examined a larger excerpt (23 sentences) from James' *The Portrait of a Lady* and has described a number of "transitional devices" which come close to the categories listed under the heading of cohesion in the present study. The study undertaken by Moss demonstrates that an appropriate alignment

---

lished by Routledge and Kegan Paul, London), one whole section of which will be devoted to the study of cohesion in the data examined (personal communication, July, 1973). For reference to Halliday's and Hasan's joint work on cohesion see footnote 41.

[55] Thomas H. Crowell, "Cohesion in Bororo Discourse", *Linguistics* 104, 15-27.

[56] Richard Ohmann, "Generative Grammars and the Concept of Literary Style", *Word* 20, 424-439.

[57] Eugene Nida, *Toward a Science of Translating* (Leyden, 1964), 68.

[58] One ought not, however, as Ohmann appears to do, underestimate literary sophistication nor what can be covered by "the tattered garments of traditional grammar" (cf. Ohmann, "Generative Grammars", 262).

[59] Leonard Moss, "Transitional Devices in Henry James", *The CEA Critic* 22.2.

of categories of grammatical and rhetorical description can account
for much of the connectedness of discourse as well as the style of
the text. While the present study attempts to follow the principles
of linguistic description it also takes account of the work of competent and linguistically sensitive literary scholars.[60]

Studies of lexical cohesion are much less well developed than
are those mentioned which deal mainly with grammatical cohesive
relations. However, two stylistic studies should be mentioned in
this connection. Geoffrey Leech's linguistic discussion of Dylan
Thomas' poem "This bread I break",[61] in addition to describing
some grammatical and phonological features of the poem's cohesion, deals with some aspects of lexical cohesion. Richard Handscombe's exploration of lexical ambiguities in George Herbert's
"The Collar"[62] points up the complexity of lexical structure in one
kind of poetic text and has important implications for the study
of lexical cohesion.

1.4.6. Cohesion and discourse structure

Cohesive relations, which obtain on the grammatic stratum, can
be observed and studied with the tools of descriptive linguistics
that are available at present. A good understanding of these relations in a text ought to help us in reconstructing the text's discourse
structure since cohesive relations are manifestations of that structure. The acceptance of the stratificational view of the organization
of language allows us to see cohesion as distinct from discourse
structure but nevertheless related to it and thus saves us from the

---

[60] In this connection see also Levenston's examination of cohesive devices in
his stylistic discussion of narrative technique in *Ulysses*. E. A. Levenston,
"Narrative Technique in *Ulysses:* A Stylistic Comparison of 'Telemachus' and
'Eumaeus'", *Language and Style* 5, 260-275.
[61] Geoffrey Leech, "'This bread I break' — Language and Interpretation",
Review of English Literature 6.2, 66-75. Leech also uses the term "cohesion of
foregrounding" for the relation of individual foregrounded features in a given
text to one another and to the entire text (p. 70).
[62] Richard Handscombe, "George Herbert's 'The Collar': A Study in
Frustration", *Language and Style* 3, 29-37.

pitfalls common to linguistic studies which try to account for discourse structure by attempting to extend grammar to cover discourse.

It follows from the view that sees cohesion as a manifestation of discourse structure that a text, which is taken as a continuous discourse having structure, will display cohesion. This cohesion will presumably differ in kind and degree depending on how the discourse has been structured on the semologic stratum and what options have been chosen while realizing the semologic structure on the grammatic stratum. It follows further that texts may display stronger or weaker cohesion but there will be no texts without cohesion.

We will proceed, then, on the assumption that anything which is a text has cohesion. We will also assume that the selected portions of literary writings used for analysis in the study are texts or portions of texts.

1.5. PURPOSE OF THE PRESENT STUDY

It is hoped that the descriptive apparatus set forth in Chapter 3 under the heading of cohesion will provide a useful framework for linguistic studies of some parts of discourse structure in English. It is suggested that certain theoretical and methodological problems of discourse analysis can be handled satisfactorily within the framework of the discussion of cohesion. Such a discussion should also point the way to establishing, for English, the correct units and relations obtaining on the semologic stratum and thus provide some ground for constructing a comprehensive and unified model of the description of discourse structure in English.

A more immediate aim of the present study is to open some new possibilities for research in the field of the linguistic study of literary texts. In particular it is hoped that a technique can be developed and applied to the study of cohesion in such texts. It remains to be seen what the application of such a technique to the analysis of a literary work can reveal: for example, whether it will bring out some of the special properties of the texts analyzed, and conversely, whether these special properties of the texts may be accounted for, at least in part, by the patterning of cohesive factors. The literary texts themselves should provide the measure of the value of the technique.

Gleason, who defines style as "the patterning of choices made within the options presented by the conventions of the language and the literary form",[63] states also that "many stylistic problems are related not simply to grammatical options (though often rather easily stated in this way) but rather to options on the phase-boundary where grammar and semantics interact".[64] To put it in terms of the stratificational theory, we could say that many stylistic problems can be related to the realizational relationships between the semologic and the grammatic strata. Cohesion, as will be shown in Chapter 2, is closely related to these relationships. The study of cohesion in literary texts may therefore illuminate some of the stylistic features of these texts. It ought to be possible to state explicitly some of the grounds upon which a reader or a critic of a literary work bases his estimation of the work's stylistic features.

1.6. RESTRICTION OF THE LINGUISTIC DATA

The texts used for the analysis of the problem of cohesion have been restricted to literary texts of modern written English. The use of such texts has been further restricted to prose passages from fiction by two representative modern American writers, James and Hemingway. This will ensure that the study will deal with the same language, Modern American English, and its use within one literary convention, the prose of fiction.

In spite of the restricted range of the linguistic data studied, it is hoped that the conclusions about the nature of cohesion in the analyzed texts will have relevance to these texts in particular and to literary prose texts in general. Many of the findings of the present

[63]   H. A. Gleason, Jr., *Linguistics and English Grammar* (New York, 1965), 428.
[64]   H. A. Gleason, Jr., "Probings into No-Man's Land: The Marches of Linguistics, Semantics, Stylistics", unpublished lecture given at Bowdoin College, Conference on Linguistics and English Stylistics, May 4, 1967, p. 11.

study, however, will be relevant to English texts of all kinds since literary texts constitute one large part of all English texts. The study will thus have value for discourse analysis in general to the extent that written English, and in particular literary prose texts, may display linguistic structure similar to that of any other discourse in English.

THEORETICAL BASIS FOR THE STUDY
OF COHESION

2.1. GENERAL REMARKS

The stratificational model of language provides a suitable theoretical framework for descriptive work on discourse structure. It is, at present, the only published theory with a full semology which has both its own inventory and its own tactics. The unity of a text which is manifested not only in the relations of clauses in sentence structure but also in the supra-sentence phenomena suggests the existence of a deeper, unifying structure which underlies the structures of grammar. As Gleason reports, "preliminary work with several languages suggests that it is on the semological stratum that this wider unity exists".[1]

The stratificational theory provides a natural place for the linguistic phenomena studied under the heading of cohesion since cohesive relations are seen as discourse features which are present on the grammatic stratum. Some description of this theory is therefore necessary before we can proceed to the presentation of the various cohesive categories. The description of the stratificational model will be sketched only briefly and will stress those aspects of the model which are pertinent to discourse analysis in general and to cohesion in particular.[2]

---

[1] H. A. Gleason, Jr., "Probings into No-Man's Land", p. 18.
[2] For a basic description of the stratificational theory of language see the following: H. A. Gleason, Jr., "The Organization of Language: A Stratificational View", *Monograph Series on Languages and Linguistics 17*, ed. by C. I·

2.2. STRATIFICATIONAL MODEL

A language, in the sense of de Saussure's *langue*, is a system of relations. This system underlies all linguistic structures of the language. Language — in itself an abstract system — relates real world experiences (sometimes referred to as meanings) to physical sounds or graphs. The relationship which is attained through the medium of language between sounds and experiences is a very complex one.

2.2.1. *Language systems and strata*

The earlier attempts on the part of linguists to describe linguistic facts as one system or even as two have not been fully successful. The stratificational theory, as developed in recent years by Gleason, Lamb, and others,[3] views language as consisting of several systems, called STRATAL SYSTEMS, each of which is said to be associated with a STRATUM of linguistic structure.[4]

The number of strata has been postulated differently at different stages of the development of the stratificational theory from three to six. Lamb suggests that all natural languages have at least four and some may have up to six strata. English falls in the latter category. Figure 1 represents the stratal systems that have been postulated for English.

J. M. Stuart (Washington, D.C. 1964), 75-96; Lamb, *Outline of Stratificational Grammar*; Sydney M. Lamb, "Linguistic and Cognitive Networks", *Cognition, A Multiple View*, ed. by Paul L. Garvin (New York, 1970), 195-222; Sydney M. Lamb, "The Crooked Path of Progress in Cognitive Linguistics", *Monograph Series on Languages and Linguistics* 24, ed. by Richard J. O'Brien, S.J. (Washington, D.C., 1971), 99-123; David G. Lockwood, *Introduction to Stratificational Linguistics* (New York, 1972); and Taber, *The Structure of Sango Narrative*, especially pp. 45-68. Lockwood's *Introduction* is probably the best to begin with. It contains a good basic bibliography of the literature of stratificational linguistics and gives additional readings on the topics discussed in the various chapters of the book.

[3] For names and works of other proponents of stratificational linguistics see Lockwood, *Introduction*, pp. 351-365.

[4] Lamb, *Outline*, 1.

Figure 1 shows the six systems (strata) postulated by Lamb[5] and relates them to the three major language systems (major components or primary strata) under which the six can be grouped. For the purposes of this study the recognition of the three major com-

Strata (sub-strata)	*Major components of language* (primary strata)
Hypersememic Sememic	SEMOLOGY
Lexemic Morphemic	GRAMMAR (MORPHOLOGY)
Phonemic Hypophonemic	PHONOLOGY

Figure 1. The English stratal systems

ponents will be sufficient. In this we follow Gleason who in his 1968 Georgetown paper bases his discussion of discourse structure on the assumption that there are just three strata: phonology, morphology, and semology.[6] Gleason's use of the term MORPHOLOGY for the middle component is followed in this study since we use such terms as grammatical cohesion and lexical cohesion. Both these kinds of cohesion obtain within the linguistic structure of the GRAMMAR component (GRAMMATIC stratum). The use of the adjective GRAMMATICAL in connection with the discussion of the kinds of cohesion is in a narrower sense, similar to the one current in discussions of traditional grammar.

2.2.2. The three strata

Gleason describes the three major components of language, the relationship between them, and their relation to speech sounds as follows:

---

[5]   Lamb, *Outline*, 20.
[6]   Gleason, "Contrastive Analysis in Discourse Structure", 60.

The three systems, phonology, grammar, and semology, must interact with each other in complicated ways. Since every sentence must conform to the patterns of all three, it has three structures simultaneously. These somehow find their audible expression in one sequence of sounds. These sounds are not part of the structure, nor are they part of the system. They are only a medium through which structure and system can be presented to the hearer.

Behind the sounds and somehow manifested through them is a phonologic structure of successive speech sound symbols and accompanying stresses, transitions, pitches, and terminals. All these are built into syllables and various larger sequences. These units, large and small, and their interrelations, constitute the phonologic system....

In turn, behind the phonology is another structure, of morphemes, words, phrases, sentences and the multifarious relations between such units. The grammar is distinct from the sound system, but the latter in some way manifests the grammatical structures.

Again, behind the grammar is a third system, of meaning contrasts and patterns of sense organization, the semology. It is still very poorly understood. Yet we suspect that the relationship of semology to grammar is much the same as that of grammar to phonology.[7]

2.2.3. Properties of stratal systems

There are two important characteristics of the stratal systems. (1) Each stratum has its own units (inventory) and its own syntax (tactics) specifying how these units can be arranged in structures. In this sense each stratum is independent of every other stratum. (2) The relationship between strata is one of realization or manifestation. Units and structures of one stratum are NOT composed of those of the lower stratum but only realized by them.

We can take such a familiar unit of linguistic analysis as the sentence and, applying the postulates of the stratificational theory, say that it has three structures — phonologic, morphologic, and semologic. Their relationship in a sentence is primarily one of realization. As Gleason says:

---

[7]   Gleason, *Linguistics and English Grammar*, 106.

One system gives realization to another. Each system finds its own realization outside itself, in another system of the language or, just outside language in physical sound. As the attention is transferred from one system to another there is always this complex and elusive relationship, never real identity or equivalence.[8]

The size of linguistic units is closely related to the kind of structure these units typically realize (to their rank, one might say). The grammatic structure is largely confined to sentence or lesser units, whereas semologic structure (which represents discourse structure) is realized to a large extent by the supra-sentence units.

2.2.4. Strata, discourse structure, cohesion

The insights of the stratificational theory have particular importance for the description of discourse structure. It follows from the nature of the relationships between strata that it is unprofitable to attempt to account for discourse structure by simply expanding grammar to include structures larger than sentences. Discourse structure, which is conceived at the semologic stratum in terms of the units and patterns of their arrangements obtaining on that stratum, cannot be said to be composed of clauses, sentences, and groups of sentences since they are units and structures obtaining on the separate morphologic stratum. But it ought to be possible to reconstruct the semologic structures underlying discourse from a sequence of clauses and sentences since the latter realize the semologic structure. This process of reconstruction of the semologic structure, and in part of what is often referred to as 'meaning', takes place when the hearer or reader decodes what is essentially non-linguistic material, a stream of speech sounds or a linear succession of graphic signs. The study of cohesive features of a text is in this sense also the study of discourse features of the text. We could say in other words that cohesion is a manifestation of discourse structure on the morphologic stratum.

We have described so far only the basic assumptions of the

---

[8]   Gleason, *Linguistics and English Grammar*, 106.

stratificational theory. A more detailed description of the inventories and tactics of the several strata and the realization relationships between strata will not be given here for the following two reasons:

(1) We are using the stratificational model of language mainly to place our discussion of cohesion in a suitable framework of linguistic description. This framework allows us to keep apart the different kinds of linguistic features of discourse as well as to see their relationship. This means that when discussing cohesion we restrict our consideration of discourse features only to those which are morphologic, while we recognize the existence of a deeper structure — called semologic — which underlies discourse and of which cohesive relations are only manifestations.

(2) We do not avail ourselves for the most part of the terminology of the units and tactics of various strata because they are not widely known and as yet not fully developed and used in the same way by all linguists who work with the stratificational model. In particular we do not avail ourselves of the relational network notation which is very often used in (and has become associated with) stratificational descriptions of language (especially those following Sydney Lamb's version of the model).[9] It is my belief that the main force of the stratificational theory still lies in its general assumptions rather than in its descriptive detail. We can use the traditional pre-stratificational terms of descriptive linguistics since our discussion will be restricted mainly to the morphologic stratum which has always been recognized (although not always by this name) in classical descriptive linguistics.

2.3. SEMOLOGIC STRUCTURE

There is one more aspect of the stratificational theory which ought

---

[9]   Readers interested in the relational network approach and its notation may want to consult, in addition to the works mentioned in footnote 2, Peter Reich, *Symbols, Relations, and Structural Complexity* (New Haven, Conn.: 1968); Peter Reich, "Relational Networks", *Canadian Journal of Linguistics* 15, 95-110; and Peter Reich, "The English Auxiliaries: A Relational Network Description", *Canadian Journal of Linguistics* 16, 18-50.

to be discussed briefly because of its particular relevance to the problems of discourse structure, and consequently to the discussion of cohesion. It is the problem of semologic structure.

2.3.1. Gleason's model of semologic structure

Gleason's contribution to the development of stratificational theory is particularly valuable for the application of the theory to discourse analysis. In the 1968 Georgetown paper he shows a model of semologic structure which is simple enough to be described without the full presentation of the stratal systems.[10] He postulates two classes of linguistic units for the semologic stratum, ACTIONS and CONNECTIONS. These units can be arranged in long chains according to the stratum's tactics. "We will call such a chain of Actions joined by appropriate Connections in the way required by the tactics of the language an Event-Line."[11] Figure 2 is an abstract representation of a common type of EVENT-LINE.[12]

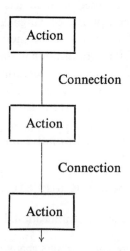

Figure 2. An abstract representation of a common type of event-line

[10]   Gleason, "Contrastive Analysis in Discourse Structure", 48-54. The model is designed to account for the typical discourse structure of narratives. It is

It must be stressed that when we talk about the units of the semolog-ic stratum they are not to be confused with the familiar grammat-ical units which have no place in the semologic structure. Although Actions will be realized most often by verbs on the morphologic stratum, Actions must not be confused with verbs. But, as Gleason writes, "Sometimes an Action on the Event-Line may be realized outside the verb, as in English *He took a walk.*, where the action is certainly what is realized as *walk*, a noun complement, rather than as *took*."[13]

Both Actions and verbs are abstract linguistic concepts, but the former are abstractions of a different kind than the latter and there-fore we cannot identify Actions with verbs, even though there may often exist a one-to-one relation between them. For example, Gleason suggests that in English the verbs *break* and *tear* realize the same Action.[14] If the affected is a stick, the verb *break* is auto-matically selected in preference to *tear*, but the opposite selection is just as automatically made if the affected is cloth. This is a language-bound feature and languages with identical or very similar semologic structures may realize those structures lexically in different ways.

The series of Actions on the Event-Line can be seen as the backbone of a narrative. All other parts of semologic structure are organized around it. For simplicity of presentation we will include in our model only one more sector of discourse structure, the participants. Gleason writes the following in this connection:

---

assumed here that a model of the semologic structure for other types of discourse would be similar in its basic features.

[11]   Gleason, "Contrastive Analysis in Discourse Structure", 48.

[12]   Representations in Figures 2, 3, and 4, as well as the other selections from "Contrastive Analysis in Discourse Structure" by H. A. Gleason, Jr. which appear in this chapter, are reprinted with the kind permission of the publishers from *Georgetown University Monograph Series on Languages and Linguistics* (= *Monograph* 21, *Report of the 19th Annual Round Table Meeting*) (Washington, D.C., 1968), 39-63.

[13]   Gleason, "Contrastive Analysis in Discourse Structure", 48.

[14]   Gleason, "Contrastive Analysis in Discourse Structure", 49.

Participants are semologic constituents of narratives related to some or all of the Actions by Roles. There is in any language a small set of such Roles, perhaps a dozen. 'Agent', 'goal', 'beneficiary', 'affected', 'causer' are appropriate labels. We must distinguish semologic roles from grammatic functions within clauses, such as subject, direct object, or indirect object. The Roles join totally different units, and they do not relate in any simple way to grammatic functions. In English, for example, a clause subject may represent almost any one of the Roles that the language distinguishes.[15]

The author then gives a diagram of typical semologic structure of narrative which takes account of only the Event-Line and the Participants. The diagram is given in Figure 3.[16]

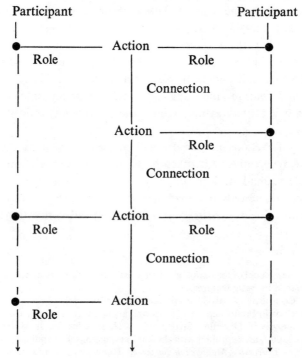

Figure 3. Typical semologic structure of a narrative (event-line and participants only)

[15]   Gleason, "Contrastive Analysis in Discourse Structure", 50. It is interesting

The diagram in Figure 3 differs from Figure 2 in that PARTICIPANTS and their ROLES have been added to the Event-Line. Participants are represented by dashed lines which are parallel to the Event-Line. This is only a graphic convention since the dashed line has the topologic properties of a point. What it really means is that each participant should be represented as a dot with lines joining it to the Actions concerned. Extending the dot into a line parallel to the event-line results in a clearer diagram. The solid lines with labels are called VALENCES. They represent relations between Action and Participant or Action and Action. The diagram has been drawn to suggest that actions differ as to how many and what Roles they permit or require. Actions which underlie such English verbs as *snow* and *rain* require none. The English grammar, however, requires that every verb have a subject and so an empty subject is supplied (e.g. *It snowed*) which does not realize any role. Other actions require from one to three roles. The manner in which these roles can be realized is complex. For example, as Gleason points out,

the Role realized by the object of *please* is realized as the subject of *like*, while the subject of *please* and the object of *like* realize the same Role. The two verbs, themselves, realize either the identical Action, or two that are very similar — that is, sharing most components. This accounts for the fact that *John likes opera.* and *Opera pleases John.* are in some sense paraphrases.[17]

---

to compare parallel developments in systemic grammar in regard to Halliday's discussion of "transitivity functions" (including "transitivity roles" such as "process", various "participant roles", "circumstance") and "transitivity clause types". Cf. Halliday, "Transitivity and Theme" and Halliday, "Language Structure and Language Function". The developments in generative-transformational grammar in the last few years point also to the need for distinguishing semantic roles from syntactic categories. Charles Fillmore's "Case Grammar" is an early example of such development. What came to be known as 'Generative Semantics' represents more recent developments of transformational theory in this direction. Cf. Fillmore "The Case for Case", and, for a discussion of later developments, Langendoen, *Essentials of English Grammar*, especially Chapters 3 and 4, pp. 32-51 and 59-88.

[16]   Gleason, "Contrastive Analysis in Discourse Structure", 51.
[17]   Gleason, "Contrastive Analysis in Discourse Structure", 51.

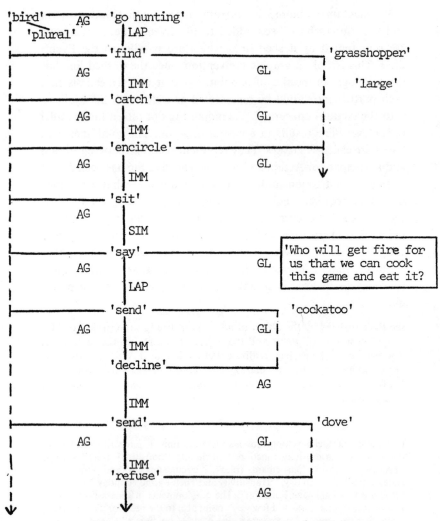

Figure 4. The event-line and the participants of a Kâte text

Gleason diagrams the Event-Line and the Participants of a Kâte text in the manner shown in Figure 4.[18]

18 Gleason, "Contrastive Analysis in Discourse Structure", 52. Kâte is a non-Melanesian language spoken in the Huon Peninsula of New Guinea.

In the diagram shown in Figure 4 Kâte's semological units are represented by the English glosses. The valences used to indicate the relations between pairs of actions and participants and actions should be interpreted in the following way:

IMM   Action B follows immediately after Action A
LAP   Action B follows after Action A with an appreciable lapse of time
SIM   Action B starts while Action A is still underway
AG   Participant A is the Agent of Action B
GL   Participant A is the goal of Action B

Figure 4 is not a full representation of the semologic structure of the Kâte text. Other features, e.g. time, have been omitted. But we can reconstruct from it the drift of the story[19] and it allows us to see something of the way Kâte orders discourse at the deepest structural level. The diagram in Figure 4 is also suggestive for English although it is to be expected that some semologic valences and units will be different for Kâte and for English.

---

[19]   Gleason gives the following English rendition of the part of the story diagrammed in the Figure 4 ("Contrastive Analysis in Discourse Structure", 53):

> (One day) the birds went hunting.
> When they had hunted a long time
> they found a large grasshopper
> they caught it.
> When they had caught it
> they encircled it
> they sat
> they said 'Who will get fire for
>   us so that we can cook this
>   game and eat it?'
> When they had asked this for a
> long time
> they sent the cockatoo
> but he declined.
> When he had declined
> they sent the dove
> but he refused.

2.3.2. Semologic structure and cohesion

The discussed model of semologic structure has the form of a RETICULUM (network) of semologic units. It is generated by the semotactics (the tactics of the semologic stratum) in such a way that an event-line (and other structures built around it) is generated by continuous accretion at the end. The generation of clauses and sentences then follows (usually closely behind the generation of the SEMOLOGIC RETICULUM) and it conforms to the requirements of the semologic structure. Two kinds of tactics are involved in this generation: semologic and grammatic tactics. This explains why certain grammatical choices which can be made in the generation of an isolated clause may not be possible for a clause within a discourse since the configurations in the semologic reticulum determine that choice. Conversely, when we examine the clauses (sentences) of a text we ought to be able to determine the semologic structure (or part of it) of the text, and consequently its discourse structure, by establishing what grammatical choices were taken in the generation of clauses. In this way we posit a close relationship between the patterning of cohesive features of discourse and the semologic reticulum of a text.

Gleason's comments in connection with the model of semologic structure presented above indicate the usefulness of the model as a basis for the systematic examination of some of the discourse features which are dealt with in this study under the heading of cohesion. In the pre-publication version of the paper on "Contrastive Analysis in Discourse Structure", Gleason describes the way participants are dealt with in the Kâte text as follows:

'Birds' is realized once, in the first clause, by a noun phrase. Thereafter, anaphora and a related grammatical device identify 'the birds' as participating in those actions where they have been diagrammed as doing so. Each of the other three participants, similarly, is specified by a noun or noun phrase once, and in the second or third involvement is indicated by similar devices. An equivalent English discourse would use pronouns in many clauses. In Kâte the more usual device is the absence of a clause constituent, sometimes called "zero anaphora".[20]

[20]   This quote is taken from a mimeographed text of the paper prepared by

In this study a number of grammatical devices supplying cohesion are exponents of anaphora. In English anaphora plays an important role in the identification of participants. As Gleason has pointed out, this identification of participants is "a true discourse feature, usually operating over stretches much longer than a single sentence".[21] The use of various grammatical and lexical devices for the identification of participants is an example of the relationship between the problems of cohesion and the larger questions of discourse structure.

There is a growing literature on discourse structure based on the stratificational model, e.g. Taber's *The Structure of Sango Narrative*, Cromack's *Language Systems and Discourse Structure in Cashinawa*, and Stennes' *The Identification of Participants in Adamawa Fulani*. In this literature the terminology pertaining to the semologic structure differs in some points from that of Gleason's as presented here. The differences, however, are minor and they do not change the basic theory.

Taber recognizes several units of the sememic stratum (which in his treatment compares to Gleason's semologic stratum). They are, from the highest rank to the lowest: the text, the text block, the event cluster, the semon, the sememe.[22] We mention this in order to elaborate on two more aspects of the semologic structure which are suggestive for the purposes of our study of cohesion.

The absence of the sentence at the semologic stratum is significant. It follows from the fact that the sentence is a unit of grammar and has no place in the semology. The clause is also a unit of grammar, although it is suggested that one of the sememic units just listed, the event-cluster, is often realized by a clause. But the match need not be one-to-one. For example, in Kâte the number of clauses, according to Gleason, usually exceeds the num-

---

H. A. Gleason, Jr., for Georgetown University 19th Annual Round Table Meeting on Linguistics and Language Studies, Washington, D.C., March 1968, p. 19. It does not appear in the published version of the paper.

[21]   Gleason, "Contrastive Analysis in Discourse Structure", 53.

[22]   Taber, *Structure of Sango Narrative*, 91.

ber of event clusters, perhaps by 50 percent.[23] In our diagram, a part of the reticulum, which consists of an action together with the attached participants and valences, will represent an event cluster.

We have mentioned the concept of the event cluster because it is one of the insights of stratificational theory which is particularly suggestive for the present study. It permits us to relate a unit of semology with that of grammar. Let us illustrate from Cromack[24] by discussing a short sememic reticulum (see Figure 5).

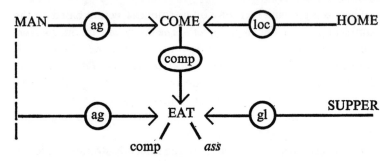

Figure 5. An example of a short sememic reticulum

There are some differences in notation and a few more details but they are not likely to cause confusion. The abbreviations *ag* and *gl* mark the same valences as those in Gleason's diagram. The abbreviation *comp* is to be interpreted as "Event A is completed (before B)", *ass*, as "Event A is asserted", and *loc*, as "A is a complement of location". We should note here that *IMM*, *SIM*, and *LAP* are a specifically Kâte set; all we can expect in another language is a similar set, not a similar specific list.

The diagram in Figure 5 of the semologic reticulum is given by Cromack as underlying either of two sentences *A man came home and ate supper.* or *After he came home, the man ate supper.* We can make several observations in connection with the sentences and their underlying semologic reticulum.

The two sentences are paraphrases realizing the same semologic

23   Personal communication.
24   Cromack, *Language Systems*, 44.

structure since English grammar allows that structure to be realized morphologically in more than one way. The two event-clusters are realized by two clauses,[25] each time with a one-to-one relation. However, the pairs of clauses realizing the same event-cluster in the two sentences are different. They differ in the way the participant MAN is realized in them and in the manner of their connection. In the first sentence MAN is realized only once — in the first clause — by a noun phrase. It is not realized in the second clause of the sentence where we have a case of zero anaphora. In the second sentence MAN is realized twice, once in each clause. An anaphoric item, the pronoun *he*,[26] is used in the first clause and the

[25]   According to the view taken in this study, the sentence *A man came home and ate supper.* contains two clauses. This is the "zero anaphora" interpretation and can be diagrammed as in (a).

(a)

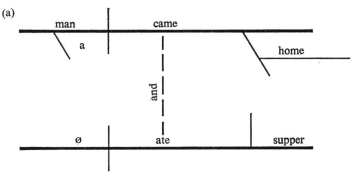

Not every grammarian would call the above sentence two clauses. The traditional interpretation would consider the sentence as containing a compound predicate. The diagram would then be as in (b).

(b)

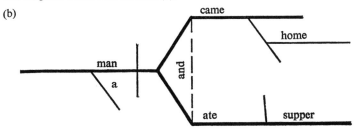

[26]   The pronoun *he* is, in fact, both anaphoric (in relation to the larger discourse

noun phrase, *the man*, is used in the second to realize the same participant. The clauses of the first sentence are joined in a coordinate construction and those of the second sentence in a subordinate one. Different connectors, *and* and *after*, are used. We would also propose that the first event-cluster may be realized by a grammatical construction which is not a clause. Three such constructions are suggested. The resultant sentences would read: *Having come home the man ate supper*; *After returning home the man ate supper*; and *On his return home the man ate supper*.

One of the conclusions from the above discussion of Cromack's example of a semologic reticulum would be that the same sememic structures may be realized by a variety of grammatical forms. This, together with the previous observation that certain configurations in the semologic reticulum may determine the choice of the grammatical form, leads us to conclude that the realizational relations between the semologic and morphologic strata are complex. To add further to the complexity of the inter-stratal relations we can quote Cromack who writes: "It is clear that grammatical forms are involved in signalling multiple semologic features, often simultaneously."[27]

This complex nature of the realizational relationships between the semologic and morphologic strata calls for extreme caution when drawing any conclusions about the semologic structure from the patterning of cohesive features.

We have discussed the semologic stratum more than the other strata because of its dominant role in generating discourse structures. But it is important to remember that all three systems are involved in generating discourse — semology, morphology, and phonology — each with its relevant patterns extending throughout the discourse. There are, then, three kinds of features that characterize discourse: semologic, morphologic (or grammatic) and phonologic discourse features. The latter are not mentioned here

---

which must be presupposed as the context of that sentence) and cataphoric (in relation to its function within the sentence).
[27]   Cromack, *Language Systems*, 71-72.

not only because the study deals with written texts but, more important, because they are not of direct interest in this book.

The discourse features we are examining in this study of cohesion are those obtaining on the morphologic (grammar) stratum. They have to be seen against the background of the deeper, semologic structure underlying discourse.

The discussion of the stratal systems — and especially of the semologic stratum — allows us to perceive the nature of cohesive relations and gives them a place in a comprehensive model of language. Cohesive relations can be given a place in the stratificational model if a semologic structure is seen underlying the morphologic (grammatic)[28] features of discourse.

[28] That is 'grammatical' and 'lexical' features, to use more traditional terminology.

3

DESCRIPTIVE FRAMEWORK FOR THE
STUDY OF COHESION

In this chapter a number of cohesive categories will be discussed. However, before proceeding to the discussion of the various categories we must note one important cohesive factor which is often taken for granted and passed over without any mention. Yet this frequently overlooked linguistic feature of any text carries much of the burden of what results in the cohesion of clauses and sentences.

3.1. ORDER AS COHESIVE FACTOR

The order in which sentences follow one another in a text is an important feature in the recognition of a group of sentences as a text. This can be testified to by the fact that speakers of a language, when presented with any assembly of sentences following one another — even when those sentences have been chosen from various distant parts of a text and put together randomly, will try as hard as they can to impose some interpretation on the whole. Simply by virtue of their appearing in a certain order together, the assumption is made that the collection of sentences is a text. If he does it at all, it usually takes the reader quite a while to abandon his attempts to treat the conglomeration of sentences as a text.[1]

[1] Such a conglomeration of twelve sentences randomly assembled from a short story was prepared. Every third and eleventh sentence from several consecutive pages of Hemingway's "Big Two-Hearted River: Part I" was copied and then these sentences were typed out following one another (in the graphic arrange-

As early as 1921, Sapir had noticed this linguistic phenomenon and stressed its importance. He remarked that the most fundamental and the strongest of all "methods of relating word to word and element to element, in short, of passing from the isolated notions symbolized by each word and by each element to the unified proposition that corresponds to a thought" is the method of order.[2] What Sapir says of the function of order in language structure in relation to words may also have relevance for clauses and sentences.

---

ment of a paragraph), once in the original order in which they appeared in the story and the second time they were all shifted randomly. Both these pseudo-texts were given to students in a college English composition class with the instruction to comment on them in regard to their meaning and structure. The students tried to interpret the sentences as a whole or at least several sentences in a group. They tried also to rearrange them, improve anaphora, transitions, etc. so that the sentences made more sense. Only a few recognized finally that they were not examining a text but a group of unconnected sentences. Interestingly enough, many of the grammatical and lexical signals they were searching for in order to explicate those supposed passages were of the kind studied here as cohesive features. Most tried to reconstruct the non-existent semologic structure of the whole, without success, although they were usually able to read some meaning into a sequence of two or three sentences. None were able to give any consistent interpretation of the passages as a whole. There were a few students who did not even consider that giving a consistent interpretation of the whole passage might be an impossible task. The students' comments did not differ much in the case of each of the two sets of sentences, except that the second time some began to suspect they were being used in an experiment.

Although the evidence of this experiment and of several others where texts with purposely mangled cohesion were used is strongly suggestive of the importance of cohesive relations for the interpretation of connected discourse, it is not presented here as any material evidence. These experiments are quite incidental to the purpose of this study and have suggestive value only.

[2] Edward Sapir, *Language* (New York, 1921), 110-111. Sapir illustrates this relating method of order by asking the reader to think of three "ideas" — a color, a person or thing, and an action — and to set down a symbol of each (*red, dog,* and *run*). He then proceeds to discuss the manner in which English speakers would relate the three symbols — *red dog run* — and the speakers' sensitivity to such "syntactic adhesions" as the "attributive relation of quality", the "subjective relation", and the "attributive relation of circumstance". One of his conclusions is, "Words and elements, then, once they are listed in a certain order, tend not only to establish some kind of relation among themselves but are attracted to each other in greater or less degree."

The order in which clauses and sentences follow in a text is, then, a cohesive factor which is always present in the text and which in combination with other cohesive factors — and sometimes even alone — indicates what kind of cohesive relations obtain among the sentences and clauses. Since this order is a necessary feature of any text we will not mention it every time a group of sentences is analyzed for cohesion. But it will underlie implicitly correlations involving all other cohesive factors studied here. For example, we cannot examine the cohesive function of connectors without accounting for the order in which elements follow. It was noted by Ryle that (1) *She took arsenic and fell ill* and (2) *She fell ill and took arsenic* do not mean the same thing.[3] The interpretation of the cohesive function of *and* is different for (1) and (2) and depends on the order of the clauses.

3.2. COHESIVE FEATURES

It would be difficult to set up a definitive list of the various grammatical and lexical features which, in addition to the factor of order (sequence) of items, can be considered in a study of cohesion. The list of COHESIVE FEATURES AND THEIR EXPONENTS given in Figure 6 is suggestive only and by no means exhaustive. The features have been divided into two groups, GRAMMATICAL and LEXICAL, following Halliday's original classification. Numerals mark the grammatical and lexical phenomena which are considered cohesive and lower-case letters are used for the exponents of these phenomena.

The listing of cohesive features presented in Figure 6 follows in essence the listing of what Halliday referred to as the principal categories subsumed under the heading of cohesion. The two listings differ, however, in the manner of classification and in some details.

---

[3] G. Ryle, *Dilemmas* (Cambridge, 1954), 118. Quoted after J. F. Staal, "'And'", *Journal of Linguistics* 4, 79. Incidentally, this raises the question of there being more than one connector represented homonymously as *and* (cf. Staal, "'And'", 79-81) or of *and* being a minimally marked connector.

A. Grammatical
   1. Anaphora and cataphora
      (a) pronouns
         (i)   personal pronouns, e.g. *he, him, she, it, they*
         (ii) demonstrative pronouns: *this, these, that, those*
         (iii) relative pronouns: *who, which, that, whom, whose*
      (b) determiners: *the, this, these, that, those*
      (c) personal possessives, e.g. *his, its, their*
      (d) substitutes
         (i)   verbal (*do*)
         (ii) nominal (*one*)
         (iii) partial
      (e) adverbs, e.g. *there, then*
      (f) submodifiers, e.g. *such, so*
   2. Coordination and subordination
      (a) connectors
   3. Enation and agnation
      (a) enate sentences
      (b) agnate sentences

B. Lexical
   1. Repetition of item
   2. Occurrence of synonym or item formed on same root
   3. Occurrence of item from same lexical set (co-occurrence group)

Figure 6. Cohesive features and their exponents

Halliday's distinction between structural and non-structural categories has been omitted here since structural (in the narrow sense of the term) relations between clauses of a sentence are not studied here unless they are also signalled by connectors. As for the categories of enation and agnation, they could not come under the heading of structural cohesion in the narrow sense since they refer to inter-sentence relations.[4]

---

[4] Halliday defines structure as "the ordered arrangement of one or more items of the same rank to form an item of the rank above" (the ways in which morphemes are organized into words, words into groups, groups into clauses,

Following the policy of excluding purely structural relations of clauses from this investigation, Halliday's original categories of dependence and linking have also been left out of our listings of cohesive features. Instead the features of COORDINATION and SUBORDINATION have been introduced.[5] These are meant to designate a range of phenomena which is both narrower and wider than the relation of clauses in sentence structure. Connectors can now be listed as exponents of the features of coordination and subordination. This results in a more unified listing of the grammatical features of cohesion and is an improvement from the point of view of the explicitness of the grammatical items for which a text has to be examined to determine its cohesive features.

It is not possible, however, to list, in a parallel way, the features and exponents of lexical cohesion. There are at present no ready terms in linguistics which could be used to designate the phenomena studied under the heading of the lexical features of cohesion.

Anaphora has been broadened to include cataphora. The latter is not considered cohesive by Halliday.[6] But in the present study

---

and clauses into sentences). Cf. Halliday, "The Linguistic Study of Literary Texts", 303-304. All these arrangements could be considered cohesive but we have restricted our study of cohesion in regard to such structures only to those of the highest rank and only if the organization of clauses into sentences involves connectors. Anaphora, of course, accounts also for relations of clauses in sentences.

[5] Halliday uses the term "co-ordination" instead of "linking" in his revised version of "The Linguistic Study of Literary Texts", reprinted in *Essays on the Language of Literature*, ed. by Seymour Chatman and Samuel R. Levin (Boston, 1967), 218-219. His use of the terms "dependence" and "co-ordination" is not to be equated with the more traditional use of the terms 'subordination' and 'coordination'. For example, Halliday's "dependence" includes non-defining (non-restrictive) relative clauses but NOT defining (restrictive) relative clauses. The latter are, in Halliday's 'scale-and-category' grammar, accounted for in the structure of the nominal group (they become Q elements by rank shift). Cf. M. A. K. Halliday, "Categories of the Theory of Grammar", *Word* 17, 241-292.
[6] Halliday, "The Linguistic Study of Literary Texts", 304. Hasan, on the other hand, recognizes instances where demonstratives can function cohesively when used cataphorically (even though she restricts her use of the term cohesion to relations between and among sentences). Cf. Ruqayia Hasan, *Grammatical Cohesion*, 59-61 (cf. discussion of *this* and *here*).

certain occurrences of cataphoric relations are seen as cohesive. Halliday's substitution has been included under the heading of anaphora since it represents essentially the same cohesive relation. It is preserved in (d) by its exponents, verbal and nominal substitutes. Anaphora, including its special manifestation, zero anaphora, and cataphora are discussed in detail in section 3.3. Enation and agnation are a new category added to the list of cohesive features. They will be discussed in section 3.5.

Other differences with Halliday's original listing are concerned mainly with detail. "Deictics" have been replaced by two more specific terms, determiners and the personal possessives. Pronouns have been specified as the personal pronouns and the demonstrative pronouns. The latter are not listed by Halliday. Adverbs are listed here with other exponents of anaphora. Halliday mentions them only in his subsequent discussion of cohesive factors.

The listing of lexical cohesive features has been expanded by addition of "occurrences of synonym or item formed on the same root". It is possible that Halliday's "occurrence of item from same lexical set" is intended to include also the latter phenomena. In any case the listing given in Figure 6 seems more specific and explicit and therefore will be easier to apply to the study of cohesion.

The listing of cohesive features used here has been set up differently from that suggested by Halliday for two reasons. This present listing will achieve a greater consistency with the theory of cohesion presented. It will also provide a workable descriptive framework for the examination of texts for the purpose of establishing their cohesive features.

Using the framework described in this chapter, a text is scanned for the grammatical items which are listed as exponents of cohesive features and each occurrence of such items is marked in the text. Then the function of each item is examined in order to establish whether this function is in fact cohesive and which elements of the text cohere because of the presence of such items. The patterns of grammatical cohesive relations can then be drawn and a numerical account of the grammatical cohesive items and relations can be given.

The examination of the lexical cohesive features can then proceed in a similar way. However, our descriptive framework is weaker in this part and does not allow the same degree of explicitness and precision which characterizes the grammatical part. Too little work has been done in this field to allow a better statement of the problem of lexical cohesion. As Halliday writes, "a valid assessment of lexical cohesion depends on the study of collocations in very large samples of text, this being necessary to the recognition of lexical sets; work of this kind on English texts is only just beginning."[7]

We will have fewer explicit leads therefore in searching for lexical cohesive features. The intuition of the language user will be called upon more often and the results of our analysis may not always be fully valid here. But we cannot omit consideration of lexical cohesion from this study since both kinds of cohesive features determine in conjunction what is studied here as cohesion. The statements about one are often not full or even valid without the consideration of the other. The two kinds of features are often found in some kind of combination.

Statements about the kinds of cohesion a text displays and their relative degrees can then be made following the analytic work described above and in Chapter 4.

3.3. ANAPHORA

Anaphora is probably that cohesive feature which has received the most attention in classical descriptive linguistics although its implications for the grammatical relations obtaining in structures larger than sentences were often overlooked or just not stressed enough. For example, Bloomfield devoted a whole chapter in his

---

[7]   Halliday, "The Linguistic Study of Literary Texts", 305. There has been little work done on lexis since Halliday wrote the paper. John McH. Sinclair's essay "Beginning the Study of Lexis" is still probably the best source of information about such work. Cf. John McH. Sinclair, "Beginning the Study of Lexis", *In Memory of J. R. Firth*, ed. by C. Bazel *et al.* (London, 1966), 410-430.

Language to the discussion of "Substitution", much of which is concerned with anaphora. The author introduces the discussion of anaphoric substitutes as follows:

To a large extent, some substitution-types are characterized, further, by the circumstance that the form for which substitution is made, has occurred in recent speech. Thus, when we say *Ask that policeman, and he will tell you*, the substitute *he* means, among other things, that the singular male substantive expression which is replaced by *he*, has been recently uttered. A substitute which implies this, is an *anaphoric* or *dependent* substitute, and the recently-uttered replaced form is the *antecedent*.[8]

But Bloomfield fails to see the full implications of anaphoric bonds across sentence boundaries. This failure is the result of considering the sentence as the upper limit of grammatical analysis.

In recent years several linguists have taken a larger view of anaphora. Gleason sees anaphora as an important structural device one of whose functions is that "it serves as a signal for connectedness between clauses or sentences". He notes that only one kind of anaphora — reflexive anaphora — is restricted to single clauses and that, although every type of anaphora is restricted in some way, "most extend beyond single clauses, and operate within sentences or connected groups of sentences of various levels".[9]

The nature of anaphoric relations as essentially features of discourse structure has been noted by Halliday who, in a different context (organization of message into information units with its distinction between "given" and "new" information), writes that "in any information unit that is non-initial in a discourse, recoverable information tends to be represented anaphorically, by reference, substitution or ellipsis." He further writes that "anaphoric items are inherently 'given' in the sense that their interpretation depends on identification within the preceding text."[10]

More recently (1972) Quirk, Greenbaum, Leech, and Svartvik, in their discussion of sentence connection, have devoted considerable attention to the question of anaphora functioning across sen-

[8]   Leonard Bloomfield, *Language* (New York, 1933), 249.
[9]   Gleason, *Linguistics and English Grammar*, 344-345.
[10]   Halliday, "Transitivity and Theme", 206.

tence boundaries under the headings of "substitution", "discourse reference", "comparison", and "ellipsis".[11] That discussion, together with Ruqaiya Hasan's treatment of "reference" and "substitution",[12] provides a fairly good descriptive basis for the investigation of the various grammatical devices of inter-sentence cohesion subsumed in the present study under the heading of anaphora (and cataphora). Thus what follows in this section is only a brief discussion of the category of anaphora as it is used in this book.

Many of the grammatical items listed under the heading of anaphora may be also CATAPHORIC. Cataphora may be seen as the reverse of anaphora (or its complement), as it points forward in the text. Very frequent in this use is the definite article *the* which then signals that the defining element is coming, as in *The Confessions of Nat Turner*, where the defining element *Nat Turner* follows *Confessions*. As the latter example indicates, not all instances of cataphora will be cohesive.

The device whereby a second (or another later) involvement of a participant is indicated by the absence of a clause constituent is called in the present study ZERO ANAPHORA.[13] In the sentence *A man came home and (Ø) ate supper*, the zero, (Ø), marks the position in the second clause where an alternative grammatical construction would have the anaphoric third person pronoun *he*. We may say

---

[11]   Quirk, Greenbaum, Leech, and Svartvik, *A Grammar of Contemporary English*, Chapter Ten, especially 677-715.

[12]   Hasan, *Grammatical Cohesion*. Cf. also Ruth Crymes, *Some Systems of Substitution Correlations in Modern American English* (The Hague, 1968).

[13]   In many present-day treatments of grammar this would be considered a special case of ellipsis (or deletion). Cf., e.g. Quirk, Greenbaum, Leech and Svartvik, *A Grammar of Contemporary English*, 555. But we will use the term ZERO ANAPHORA as defined in this study because of its usefulness in designating a device for one kind of anaphoric marking of participant involvement and the fact that the term has already been introduced with such a sense in the model for discourse structure analysis discussed in Chapter 2. Cf. Gleason "Contrastive Analysis in Discourse Structure", 53. It can also be observed that if we follow the framework of stratificational grammar — whose formulations are stated in terms of relations and not processes — we need to avoid using terms like "ellipsis", even though on the whole we avail ourselves of traditional terminology for specifying grammatic relations.

that the pronoun is replaced by zero in the second clause. The instances of zero anaphora are counted as cohesive ties in the same way as the occurrences of anaphoric pronouns. The use of the term ZERO ANAPHORA in the present study is different from Hockett's use of the term.[14] The phenomena which Hockett calls "zero anaphora" will be discussed under the heading of PARTIAL SUBSTITUTES in section 3.3.5.

It should be noted that in the presentation of the anaphoric and cataphoric substitutes that follows, only those items will be discussed which mark cohesive relations between clauses and sentences. Reflexive pronouns, for example, will not be discussed.

Anaphoric and cataphoric relations will be defined and illustrated together with the other -PHORIC relations in section 3.3.3.

3.3.1. Pronouns

Three kinds of pronouns are listed here as those that may function anaphorically: the PERSONAL PRONOUNS, the DEMONSTRATIVE PRONOUNS, and the RELATIVE PRONOUNS. Certain inflectional forms of the personal pronouns, e.g. *his, their*, are listed separately as the PERSONAL POSSESSIVES. They are often treated together with other specific determiners like *this* and *that* as deictics.[15]

Of the PERSONAL PRONOUNS only the third person pronouns *he, she, it*, and *they*, together with their inflectional forms (so called objective case) *him, her*, and *them*, may function anaphorically, strictly speaking. The first and second person pronouns normally do not function anaphorically although there are contexts in

[14]   Cf. Charles Hockett, *A Course in General Linguistics* (New York, 1958), 259.
[15]   For a detailed treatment of deictics within the framework of the categories first introduced by Halliday (in 1961 in "Categories of the Theory of Grammar") see Michael Gregory, "English Patterns: Perspectives for a Description of English", mimeographed preliminary version (Toronto, 1966), section 6, especially pp. 5-7. Gregory distinguishes six classes of deictics, with further subclasses at a greater degree of delicacy. In his classification personal possessives and rankshifted nominal groups in the possessive (subclass "possessive article reference"), the definite article (subclass "definite article reference"), and the other determiners (subclass "demonstrative reference") belong — together with four other subclasses — to the class of "deictics of simple reference".

which they could be considered anaphoric. Ruqaiya Hasan states, for example, that in written English these pronouns are anaphoric "when they occur in quoted ('direct') speech (as opposed to the writer addressing his readers)".[16] Gleason considers the type of anaphora involving the third person pronouns the most important one and says that "conversely, anaphora is the most important function of these pronouns, though not the only one".[17]

These pronouns are sometimes cataphoric, as is *they* in *They have my undying gratitude who brought me here*, and sometimes serve merely as fillers of sentence positions, as is *it* in *It is raining*.[18]

The DEMONSTRATIVE PRONOUNS *this* and *that* (and their plural forms *these* and *those*) are sometimes anaphoric, as in *Here are two eggs: this is for you, and that for me*.[19] They are treated here separately from the demonstratives *this* and *that*, which are grouped together with *the* and are called DETERMINERS.[20]

The RELATIVE PRONOUNS *who, whom, whose, which,* and *that* are

---

[16]   Hasan, *Grammatical Cohesion*, 33-34. Hasan also makes an observation that the first person plural pronoun *we* may be "intermediate" in its anaphoric function in sentences like "Mary and I were late today. We missed the early train." where some other person than the speaker (or addressee) is included in *we*.

[17]   Gleason, *Linguistics and English Grammar*, 345.

[18]   Both examples are taken from Gleason, *Linguistics and English Grammar*, 345-346.

[19]   Example taken from Hockett, *A Course in Modern Linguistics*, 258. A good example of a demonstrative pronoun functioning anaphorically as a cohesive tie between two sentences is given in Quirk, Greenbaum, Leech and Svartvik, *A Grammar of Contemporary English*, 704: "You can have two tickets for the middle of the tenth row in the theatre. *Those* are the best seats in the house."

[20]   Quirk, Greenbaum, Leech, and Svartvik in *A Grammar of Contemporary English* treat all these items under the heading of "demonstrative pronouns" but they distinguish between their "determiner" and "nominal" functions (cf. p. 217). It seems to make more sense — for the purposes of discourse structure analysis such as the study of cohesion — to separate these items in their two functions completely. Accordingly, in this study it is only in their nominal function (as heads of nominal groups) that the items, *this, these, that,* and *those* are referred to as DEMONSTRATIVE PRONOUNS. In the determiner function they are treated here simply as DETERMINERS (together with *the*). This treatment is consistent with according the genitives of personal pronouns a status separate from other pronouns, i.e. setting up a category of 'personal possessives' since they pattern in discourse much the same way as the other deictics of simple reference. Cf. footnote 15.

usually anaphoric, e.g. *My mother was the one who baked the cake* has relative *who* and antecedent *the one*.[21] Relative pronouns introduce relative clauses which can be either restrictive or non-restrictive. There are some differences in the nature and scope of the anaphoric reference of these pronouns depending on which kind of relative clause they introduce. These differences are discussed in Quirk, Greenbaum, Leech, and Svartvik.[22]

3.3.2. Determiners

The DETERMINERS *the, this* (*these*), and *that* (*those*) can be anaphoric or cataphoric. Some grammars list more items under this heading. But such items either have already been accounted for in this chapter (e.g. the personal possessives) or are of lesser importance to the study of cohesion (e.g. *a, some, any, much*). The status of the five determiners has already been discussed in section 3.3.1. in connection with demonstrative pronouns (see footnote 20).

3.3.3. Discussion of -PHORIC *relations*

While *the* may be anaphoric or cataphoric, it may also be homophoric when the noun in question is self-defining, e.g. *the moon, the army*. The term HOMOPHORIC was introduced by M.A.K. Halliday. Halliday stated in his lectures at the 1966 Linguistic Institute of the Linguistic Society of America that the anaphoric use of *the* is relatively rare (15-40 percent) and that the most frequent use of *the* is cataphoric. This fact undermines one of the most persistent myths of English — the popular notion that *the* is always anaphoric.

We have to exercise extra caution in classifying an instance of *the* as anaphoric, especially as three functions of the definite article — CATAPHORIC, ANAPHORIC, and HOMOPHORIC — are not

---

[21] Quoted from Hockett, *A Course in Modern Linguistics*, 258.
[22] Quirk, Greenbaum, Leech, and Svartvik, *A Grammar of Contemporary English*, 214-215 and 860-876. See also their discussion of *what* as a different kind of relative pronoun (p. 216).

mutually exclusive. For example, in the second sentence of *We discovered the truth at last. The truth was devastating for some of us.*, the determiner *the* is both anaphoric and homophoric.

Gleason extends such referential classes as anaphoric, cataphoric, and homophoric by adding one more class: PARAPHORIC.[23] Also in use is the term EXOPHORIC (explained below). All five possible uses of such items as *the* are diagrammed in Figure 7.

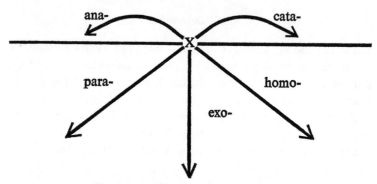

Figure 7. Explanation of -phoric relations

The symbol X in Figure 7 marks the position of a -phoric item in a text (the latter being represented by the horizontal line). The arrows above the horizontal line represent the two kinds of TEXTUAL reference (within the same text) that such an item can have and the ones below the horizontal line represent three kinds of EXTRA-TEXTUAL reference. The five -phoric relations can be explained as follows:

Anaphoric[24] — an item refers back to something else in the same

---

[23]   H. A. Gleason, Jr., class lectures, 1966.

[24]   The terms ANAPHORA and ANAPHORIC REFERENCE are well established in grammatical descriptions. There are, however, some differences in the way these terms have been defined and the way anaphoric reference has been related to deictic reference. For a discussion of some of these differences, see Crymes, *Systems of Substitution Correlations*, 21, 49n., and especially 62-63n. In transformational considerations of the sources of definite articles, anaphora is usually restricted to relations within a sentence although more recently it has

text, e.g. *the* in *A man was walking in the park. The man had a dog with him*;

Cataphoric[25] — an item refers to something coming along in the text. An excellent example of cataphoric reference is found in a sentence on page 54 of this book where three items in a row in the first clause, *he, does,* and *it,* are used cataphorically: *If he does it at all, it usually takes the reader quite a while to abandon his attempts to treat the conglomeration of sentences as a text*;[26]

Paraphoric — an item refers to something in another text, e.g. another work of art (say, an item in one of Shakespeare's plays refers to something very specific in another play of Shakespeare) expected to be known and related to the text at hand in a special way;

Exophoric — an item refers to a situation outside of language, e.g. when we say *that book* and indicate by gesture which one it is;[27]

---

been conceded by some transformational grammarians that in a pair of sentences like "I saw a cat in the tree this morning. This afternoon *the* cat was gone." *the* would be treated as anaphoric "in a discourse grammar" (but "in a sentence grammar", it would have to be treated as either "non-linguistically anaphoric" or "as having a deleted relative clause or preceding conjoined sentence"). For a fuller discussion of the preceding see Stockwell, Schachter, and Partee, *The Major Syntactic Structures of English,* 73-75ff. The use of the terms anaphora and anaphoric in the present study accords on the whole with the use of these terms in Halliday "The Linguistic Study of Literary Texts", Gleason, *Linguistics and English Grammar,* Hasan, *Grammatical Cohesion,* and Quirk, Greenbaum, Leech, and Svartvik, *A Grammar of Contemporary English.*

[25] The term CATAPHORA is not as well established as that of anaphora (the instances of what could be considered cataphora often subsumed under the heading of anaphora). For more examples and discussion of cataphora, see Halliday "The Linguistic Study of Literary Texts", 304, Hasan, *Grammatical Cohesion,* 24-25ff., and Quirk, Greenbaum, Leech and Svartvik, *A Grammar of Contemporary English,* 155 and 700-702.

[26] Quirk, Greenbaum, Leech, and Svartvik, *A Grammar of Contemporary English,* give some examples of cataphora functioning across sentence boundaries. One is as follows: "*This* should interest you, if you're still keen on boxing. The world heavyweight championship is going to be held in Chicago next June, so you should be able to watch it live." Cf. pp. 701-702.

[27] For a somewhat different (more general) use of the term "exophora", see Hasan, *Grammatical Cohesion,* 36-40 and 50-51.

Homophoric — an item refers to one's general knowledge. The reference is cultural. Homophoric items differ in the degree of how general or specific their reference is. For example, *the earth, the sun,* and *the moon* will have the same reference for everybody who understands English, whereas *the prime minister* will have the reference restricted usually to one country — say Pierre Elliot Trudeau in Canada in 1973 — and *the premier* (as the term is used in Canada), to one province — say Edward Schreyer (in Manitoba in 1973). In *The Queen arrived in Canada today* (June 25, 1973), reported by the press anywhere in the English-speaking world, Elizabeth II will be the referent of *the Queen,* but if we took as our example of homophora *the press* then the reference would be local — say the Australian press in Melbourne.[28]

Only two of the relations diagrammed in Figure 7, the ones above the horizontal line, may be cohesive since their reference is to parts of the same discourse.

3.3.4. *Personal possessives*

As in the case of personal pronouns, only the third person personal possessives, such as *his, her, its,* and *their,* may be used anaphorically, strictly speaking. But we should add that similar arguments to those given in the discussion of the personal pronouns in section 3.3.1. (see also footnote 16) could be advanced for considering some uses of the first and second person personal possessives as cohesive (i.e. anaphoric or even cataphoric).

3.3.5. *Substitutes*

This is not a satisfactory term to designate the items in this group

---

[28] Quirk, Greenbaum, Leech and Svartvik, *A Grammar of Contemporary English*, 155-156, discuss the homophoric uses of *the* but they do not use the term homophoric. They propose the term "indexical *the*" for this use of the article.

since the term anaphoric substitutes is also used here for all items studied under the heading of anaphora. It will be used, however, with one of the three adjectives specifying the subgrouping of substitutes. The three subgroups are: VERBAL SUBSTITUTES including *do* and its inflectional forms; NOMINAL SUBSTITUTES, such as *one*, *ones*, *theirs*; and PARTIAL SUBSTITUTES which are explained below.[29]

The verbal and nominal substitutes are listed by Halliday as cohesive elements but they are not considered anaphoric; they are listed separately as the phenomena of substitution. Here we recognize their essential anaphoric nature though the type of anaphora they signal is different from any of the types which have been described for pronouns. In this we follow Hockett who writes that *do* is anaphoric and explains the different nature of anaphora due to this item by pointing out that "in a sentence *He doesn't like her, but I do,* the terminal *do* has as its antecedent the phrase *does like her*; the *not* of *doesn't like her* is not part of the antecedent".[30]

Gleason stresses the difference in the kind of anaphora that is signalled by the personal pronouns and by *do*. He points out that *do*, when anaphoric, refers to a second occurrence of a similar act whereas *he*, for example, marks a second involvement of an identical participant.[31]

I have introduced the term PARTIAL SUBSTITUTE to designate those anaphoric substitute items which constitute a partial repetition

---

[29]   In the present study the term SUBSTITUTES is used for a much narrower range of grammatical features than is usual in linguistic descriptions of English which deal with substitution. For some such discussions of substitutes, see Bloomfield, *Language*, 247-263; Hockett, *A Course in Modern Linguistics*, 253-260; Robert L. Allen, "The Classification of English Substitute Words", *General Linguistics* 5, 7-20; Eugene A. Nida, *A Synopsis of English Syntax* (Norman, Oklahoma, 1960), 45-54; and Ruth Crymes, *Systems of Substitution Correlations*. Hasan — who makes a distinction between substitution and reference — and Quirk, Greenbaum, Leech, and Svartvik use the term substitution in a similar way as the term is used in this study except that their use is more inclusive. See Hasan, *Grammatical Cohesion*, 82-145, and Quirk, Greenbaum, Leech, and Svartvik, *A Grammar of Contemporary English*, 677-700.
[30]   Hockett, *A Course in Modern Linguistics*, 258.
[31]   H. A. Gleason, Jr., personal communication, 1968.

of a phrase for which they substitute. Hockett calls this kind of substitution "zero anaphora" and explains it as follows:

> The first part of *She couldn't have been thinking of me, could she*? contains the long verb phrase *could have been thinking*. In the second part of the sentence, the speaker does not use a special substitute form (like *do* or *did*), nor does he repeat the entire verb phrase; instead, he uses the first word of the verb phrase as a substitute for the whole. The rest of the verb phrase is "replaced by zero"... we say *I like fresh candy better than stale*, where an adjective, *stale*, followed by no noun at all, occurs substitutively for the phrase *stale candy*.[32]

The term partial substitutes includes the ten modal auxiliaries: *can, could, may, might, shall, should, will, would, must*, and *ought* (*to*) when they are used in reference to a previously stated verb. For example, in the sentences *They asked John if he planned to hijack a plane to Ulan Bator. John told them he might if that were the only way to get there.*, the auxiliary *might* functions as a partial substitute.[33]

3.3.6. Adverbs

Adverbs such as *there* and *then* are often anaphoric in function. For example, there is a cohesive element in the following pair of sentences because of its anaphoric character: *We went into the house. There we found John.* Similarly, *then* functions cohesively as an anaphoric substitute in *The doctor didn't arrive until early in the morning. Then it was already too late.*

It should be pointed out that a large number of adverbs which function cohesively will be studied under CONNECTORS in this book.[34]

---

[32]   Hockett, *A Course in Modern Linguistics*, 259.
[33]   Crymes, who derives these substitutes from ellipsis, calls them "representers" and classes them as "secondary substitutes". See R. Crymes, *Systems of Substitution Correlations*, 35.
[34]   Greenbaum, who deals with some of the functions of adjuncts as they are realized by adverbs (designated usually in English grammars as 'sentence modifiers', 'sentence adverbs', or 'linking adverbs', although Greenbaum does not use these terms), considers some uses of adverbs in sentence connection. Many of these are treated under the category of connectors in the present study. Cf. Sidney Greenbaum, *Studies in English Adverbial Usage* (London, 1969).

3.3.7. Submodifiers

There is a small group of anaphoric items such as *such* and *so* which have been termed "submodifiers" by Halliday.

Further study may reveal what other items can be included under this heading.[35] An example of a submodifier functioning cohesively for two sentences will be *such* in *Television often shows horror movies on children's programs. Some believe such movies are not fit for children.* The following are two more examples of submodifiers functioning cohesively across sentence boundaries.

(1) When we arrived at the Yorkdale shopping plaza, it seemed that every parking space was taken. We were surprised to find the parking lot *so* full.

(2) I asked John if he looked forward to going to law school in the fall. He said that he did *so* very much.

In the second sentence of (2) we have an example of the verbal substitute *do* functioning jointly with the submodifier *so*. That example also involves the intensifier *very much* whose cohesive function is, at least in part, lexical (through the collocation *look forward — very much*). Similarly, much of the cohesive force of *so* in (1) depends on lexical cohesion. As these examples indicate, there are borderline cases where grammatical and lexical cohesion cannot be neatly separated. But this perhaps should be considered an additional cohesive factor when the function of items like submodifiers is considered.

3.3.8. General remarks

In the discussion of the individual grammatical forms which can be anaphoric it was noted that some of them may also be cata-

[35] Hasan lists also *as, more, less, equally,* and "one or two other 'adverbs of comparison' formed from the 'adjectives of comparisons'". She notes the variation in the range of anaphoric reference of such items from "specific nominal" to "extended text" reference. See Hasan, *Grammatical Cohesion,* 74-79. See also Hasan's discussion of *so* under her category of substitution (pp. 115-125) in which she gives some examples of anaphoric *so,* one of which is: "You believe he is guilty. If so he will confess." (p. 123).

phoric and that in some cases cataphora can be cohesive. It is supposed that some other forms listed under anaphora may also be used cataphorically and function cohesively in such use. But this may be determined only by examining large portions of different kinds of text.

Anaphoric items function cohesively only when they are used unambiguously, that is, when the context shows clearly what are their antecedents. In other words, it must be possible to establish without any doubt what elements in the text are replaced or referred to by the anaphoric items. The following passage from James' *The Portrait of a Lady* illustrates that even the masters of the English language sometimes fail in this respect, and consequently the cohesion of their texts suffers in the respective parts. The anaphoric items with ambiguous antecedents have been italicized.

Madame Merle looked a moment at Isabel and at the master of the house. He was leaning against the parapet, facing *her*, his arms folded; and *she* at present was evidently not lost in the mere impersonal view, persistently as *she* gazed at it. As Madame Merle watched her *she* lowered *her* eyes; *she* was listening, possibly with a certain embarrassment, while *she* pressed the point of *her* parasol into the path. Madame Merle rose from her chair. "Yes, I think so!" she pronounced.[36]

It may be suggestive to note that a group of college students in an English composition course, when asked to mark which instances of *she* and *her* referred to Isabel and which to Madame Merle, gave answers which indicated a number of possible combinations of anaphoric reference for these items. The conclusion would be that ambiguous anaphora weakens cohesion since it is either impossible or extremely difficult to reconstruct certain important parts of the semologic structure, such as in this case participants, underlying the grammatic structure of a given passage.

---

[36]   Henry James, *The Portrait of a Lady* (New York, 1881), 267. The page number is to the edition of the novel published by Random House in *The Modern Library College Editions* (1966).

3.4. COORDINATION AND SUBORDINATION

COORDINATION AND SUBORDINATION are used in this study as cover terms for these cohesive relations that obtain between clauses as well as sentences of a text which are indicated by connectors.[37] This means that we are using these terms for not quite the same range of grammatic phenomena as the relations of clauses in the sentence structure for which these terms have been traditionally used. It is assumed here that the connectivity of two or more sentences due to the presence of connectors whose function is to link these sentences into a morphologic construction larger than a single sentence is essentially of the same kind as the grammatical connectivity, marked also by connectors, of clauses within a sentence. In other words, there is no reason — except for the arbitrarily set limits of grammatical analysis — to restrict the study of the relations of coordination and subordination, indicated by connectors, to clauses in the sentence structure. Certain types of these relations may be more typical of sentences than of clauses and vice versa, and some may obtain exclusively between either of the two grammatical units. The varying use of different connectors to indicate relations between clauses and those between sentences seems to suggest this possibility. But the fact remains that these relations are not restricted to clauses in a sentence but can also be seen in groups of sentences.

The last sentence of the preceding paragraph has been constructed clumsily to illustrate the point it makes. *But* is used twice, first as a sentence connector and then as a clause connector. In each case it indicates the same type of construction, that is, coordination. The clumsiness of the sentence is probably a stylistic matter and can be removed by changing either of the two occurrences of *but* to another connector, e.g. by using *however* in place of the first *but* or *and* instead of the second.

---

[37] These terms may be changed later on to some more suitable one or ones (perhaps more than two) pending our better understanding of the types of connection marked by various connectors and the kinds of units being connected.

3.4.1. Connectors

The cohesive relations which obtain between clauses and between sentences of a text due to the presence of connectors have been divided into two large groups following one of the several possible classifications of English connectors into the subordinating and coordinating ones. Other classifications of connectors are also possible and one such is indicated within the list of coordinating and subordinating connectors given below. The list is taken from Gleason's *Linguistics and English Grammar*.[38]

COORDINATING CONNECTORS

Cumulative or Additive: *and, likewise, moreover, in addition, furthermore*, etc.

Disjunctive: *or, nor, else, lest, otherwise, alternatively*, etc.

Adversative: *but, however, nevertheless, on the contrary, on the other hand*, etc.

Illative: *therefore, so, for this reason, then*, etc.

SUBORDINATING CONNECTORS

Causal: *because, since, as, for, for the reason that*, etc.

Purposive: *that, in order that, so that, lest, for the purposes of*, etc.

Conditional: *if, unless, provided that, whether*, etc.

Concessional: *though, although, in spite of the fact that, notwithstanding that*, etc.

Comparative: *as, than*

Temporal: *as, as soon as, while, before, until, since, when, ere*, etc.

The above classification of connectors is suggestive of the kinds of connection between clauses or sentences which are indicated by the cohesive features named here — probably very inadequately — as coordination and subordination. The relations covered by the latter two terms could be, then, grouped and named in several

---

[38] Gleason, *Linguistics and English Grammar*, 342-343.

ways, some of which might be more satisfactory than the classification used here.[39]

In this study, however, we shall use this rather general classification since it is the existence of these cohesive relations rather than their kinds that interests us. For the beginning we need a simple descriptive framework which can be applied to our preliminary study of cohesion in the selected literary texts. This framework can then be developed further in the direction which such simplified study of cohesion may indicate.

The list of connectors is not exhaustive although it would be possible to compile a complete list since connectors constitute a closed set. It serves here only as an illustrative list of the set of devices referred to generally as connectors and used to connect clauses or sentences.

Connectors function sometimes in pairs. This applies mainly to temporal connectors. For example, we have such pairs of temporals as *when... then* and *at first... then*.

3.5. ENATION AND AGNATION

ENATION and AGNATION[40] are useful categories for describing certain relations between sentences (and other constructions) which can be cohesive and which had received attention in some linguistic descriptions of English only partially under such headings as 'grammatical parallelism' and 'structural similarity'. The latter

---

[39] Some of these relations are often discussed under the headings of 'conjunction', 'conjuncts', 'disjuncts', and certain kinds of 'adjuncts'. See, for example, Lila Gleitman, "Coordinating Conjunctions in English", *Language* 41, 260-293; Robin Lakoff, "If's, and And's, and But's about Conjunction", *Studies in Linguistic Semantics*, ed. by Charles Fillmore and D. Terence Langendoen (New York, 1971), 115-149; the chapter on conjunction in Stockwell, Schachter, and Partee, *The Major Syntactic Structures of English*, 294-418. For a discussion of conjuncts, disjuncts, and adjuncts, see Greenbaum, *Studies in English Adverbial Usage*, especially the chapter on conjuncts, 36-80.

[40] The terms "enation" and "agnation" were introduced by H. A. Gleason, Jr., who describes the relations these terms denote in the chapter "Relation and Process" in *Linguistics and English Grammar*, 195-221.

terms are more or less equivalent to enation but they are open to misinterpretation or imprecise use. The terms enation and agnation are also preferable for use in this study since they are defined in terms of RELATIONS and not processes (such treatment being in accordance with the principles of stratificational linguistics where relations are the basic consideration in description of linguistic structure).

In his description of ENATION, Gleason states that "two sentences can be said to be enate if they have identical structures, that is, if the elements (say, words) at equivalent places in the sentences are of the same classes, and if constructions in which they occur are the same."[41] English literature (and here we follow Martin Joos' definition of literature[42]) is full of examples of enation functioning cohesively. We can start with nursery rhymes such as:

> This little pig went to market
> This little pig stayed home
> This little pig ate roast beef
> This little pig had none...

and move to ballads, taking as an example the following two lines from a literary ballad by Sir Walter Scott:

> He waved his proud hand and the trumpets were blown,
> The kettle-drums clashed, and the horsemen rode on...[43]

where enation of the clauses in the second line adds to their cohesion and to the cohesion of these clauses with the first clause of the first line (through partial enation). We can move then to Shakespeare and take as an example a well known passage from *Julius Caesar* in which Brutus gives his reasons for killing Caesar. Here are just a few lines to illustrate the cohesive nature of enation (the whole of that speech by Brutus contains numerous examples of cohesive enation):

[41] Gleason, *Linguistics and English Grammar*, 199.
[42] Martin Joos, *The Five Clocks* (New York, 1961), 51-52.
[43] Sir Walter Scott, "Bonny Dundee", *Anthology of Romanticism*, 3rd ed., selected, ed. by Ernest Bernbaum (New York, 1948), 54-55.

...As Caesar loved me, I weep for him; as
he was fortunate, I rejoice at it; as he was
valiant, I honour him; but, as he was ambitious,
I slew him. There is tears for his love; joy for
his fortune; honour for his valour; and death
for his ambition...[44]

As an example of this use of enation in a novel we can quote a few lines from the opening section of Sheila Watson's *The Double Hook*:

Greta was at the stove. Turning hotcakes. Reaching for the coffee beans. Grinding away James's voice.

James was at the top of the stairs. His hand half-raised. His voice in the rafters.

James walking away. The old lady falling. There under the jaw of the roof. In the vault of the bed loft. Into the shadow of death. Pushed by James's will. By James's hand. By James's words...[45]

As can be easily seen, much of the cohesion in the above passage from this modern Canadian novel depends on enation.

We can end our exemplification of enation with the Bible (which is, of course, a rich source of such examples) by quoting from Psalm 19:

The heavens declare the glory of
God; and the firmament sheweth his
handywork.
Day unto day uttereth speech, and
night unto night sheweth knowledge.[46]

As the above examples indicate, enations function cohesively often in conjunction with lexical cohesion and may be reinforced by other features of grammatical cohesion. It also should be noted that enation does not require a complete identity of grammatical structure. Sometimes enation is only partial. The complexity of the interrelations of cohesive relations under this category is considerable especially if we take into account the fact that enation is often found concurrently with agnation in some of the strongest instances of grammatical cohesion.

[44] Shakespeare, *Julius Caesar* III.ii.26-31.
[45] Sheila Watson, *The Double Hook* (Toronto, 1969), 19.
[46] *Psalm* 19:1-2.

The category AGNATION is used for relations that are opposite and complementary to enation. Gleason says that

Pairs of sentences with the same major vocabulary items, but with different structures (generally shown by differences in arrangement, in accompanying function words, or other structure markers) are agnate if the relation in structure is regular and systematic, that is, if it can be stated in terms of general rules.[47]

Following are two examples of pairs of agnate sentences:

(a) James wrote this book. $\Longleftrightarrow$ This book was written by James.

(b) She couldn't do this. $\Longleftrightarrow$ This she couldn't do.

The two-headed arrows indicate that the sentences in each pair are considered to be in a certain structural relation to each other and not a result of a transformation (process) that derives one from the other. This being the case we still need to observe that usually one of a pair of agnate sentences can be considered as basic (at least when the sentence is used out of context). We can say, for example, that *She couldn't do this* is the basic one of the pair since we feel that the order of clause elements S P C (Subject Predicator Complement) is the basic sentence pattern in English. The use of the agnate sentence *This she couldn't do* rather than *She couldn't do this* in a piece of discourse will usually be motivated by considerations which have to do with appropriate transitions from sentence to sentence. We can then say that the use of the agnate structure *This she couldn't do* is a cohesive factor in the following fragment of discourse:

There was nothing left for her but to sell the old family house. This she couldn't do.

A good literary example of agnation functioning cohesively can be found in the following opening lines from the short story "How the Whale Got his Throat" by Rudyard Kipling:

---

[47]   Gleason, *Linguistics and English Grammar*, 202.

In the sea, once upon a time, O my Best Beloved, there was a Whale, and he ate fishes. He ate the starfish and the garfish, and the crab and the dab, and the plaice and the dace, and the skate and his mate, and the mackerel and the pickerel, and the really truly twirly-whirly eel. All the fishes he could find in all the sea he ate with his mouth — so!...[48]

The second sentence of the passage follows the usual S P C pattern, except that the complement is an unusually long one (or perhaps it would be better to say that it is a series of C elements strung together) containing a list of the kinds of fish the whale ate. After this the order C P S (A) of the third sentence exemplifies a choice of an agnate sentence which results in stronger cohesion of the second and third sentences. The complement "All the fishes he could find in all the sea" naturally fits in that front position in the sentence functioning as a linking, summarizing, resumptive device after the list of fishes.

Another observation which can be made about the third sentence of Kipling's short story is that the sentence itself combines enation and agnation which can be seen as contributing to the cohesion within that sentence. The order C S P A (A standing for an adjunct element) of the sentence is mirrored by the same order of elements of the rankshifted clause which constitutes the sentence's C element. Here we have enation and agnation functioning concurrently.

The opening three lines from Dylan Thomas' "Light Breaks Where No Sun Shines" provide another example of a complex interaction of enation and agnation resulting in tight cohesion of these lines:

> Light breaks where no sun shines;
> Where no sea runs, the waters of the heart
> Push in their tides;...[49]

3.6. LEXICAL COHESION

Lexical repetition across sentence boundaries which helps to relate

---

[48]   Rudyard Kipling, *Just-So-Stories For Little Children* (Garden City, N.Y., 1927), 3. This passage was suggested to me by H. A. Gleason, Jr.
[49]   Dylan Thomas, *Collected Poems* (New York, 1953), 29.

various sentences in a text is usually evident in parts of or even in whole texts. Occurrence of the same lexical items or of synonyms or other members of the same co-occurrence class (lexical sets) in two or more adjacent or not too distant sentences can be cohesive under certain circumstances. Lexical items are understood, as it has been stated by Halliday, "to exclude closed-system items, those which occur as the unique realization of a grammatical feature and thus form one-member classes".[50] Thus all the items studied under grammatical cohesion as well as other closed-system items like prepositions will be excluded from consideration in the examination of the lexical features of cohesion.

The clearest instance of lexical cohesion occurs when the same lexical item is found in two or more adjacent clauses or sentences in the same sense. For example, in *Tomorrow would be the party. She had dreamed of that party for weeks.*, the word *party* is such a lexical item. It is essential, of course, that the two occurrences of *party* be the same lexical item. In the pair of sentences which follows the second occurrence of the homonymous lexical item *party* does not contribute to cohesion of the two sentences (not at least under the category of lexical cohesion discussed here).

She danced all night at a *party* and came home so tired she slept till noon. That was unfortunate because she had promised to spend the next morning electioneering for her *party*.[51]

Lexical cohesion can also result from the repetition of a lexical item in two or more clauses (sentences) which, although not adjacent, are in close proximity. How far apart such clauses can be and still be said to display lexical cohesion is an empirical question. The reader's ability to remember a lexical item and to associate it with another occurrence of the same item later on in the text might provide a criterion for stating how distant clauses can be and still display lexical cohesion.[52] The texts analyzed in this

[50]   M. A. K. Halliday, "Transitivity and Theme", 207.
[51]   Incidentally, the example is indicative of the difficulties one may encounter in working out a program for a computer-aided study of lexical cohesion.
[52]   Obviously, certain lexical items are remembered much longer than others.

study are short enough that we may assume that any such repetition will be cohesive.

The above statement of lexical cohesion due to the repetition of the same item has to be qualified. Not every lexical item when repeated may be considered cohesive. High-frequency items such as *get, put,* or *say* will have to be excluded from this category unless they are reinforced by some other cohesive factor. Low-frequency items, e.g. *ice-rink, excavate, prisoner, hermit,* etc. will qualify, if repeated, as cohesive factors. The question of the frequency of a lexical item is a relative one and depends on the kind of text in which the item is found.

The occurrence of a lexical item in one clause and then of its synonym in another under similar circumstances as those stated for the repetition of the same lexical item is also considered cohesive. A lexical item formed on the same root may have cohesive properties similar to those of a synonym. For example, *marriage* will cohere with *marry* just as *matrimony* coheres with *marriage.* De Saussure justified the grouping of such words as *marriage* and *marry* on the basis of what he called "associative relations" obtaining between such items. He cites examples *enseignement* 'teaching', *enseigner* 'teach', and *enseignons* '(we) teach'.[53]

There are instances of lexical cohesion which depend neither on the repetition of a lexical item nor on the occurrence of synonyms or words having a common root. They are due to the occurrence of lexical items belonging to the same lexical set or to what might be called a co-occurrence group. Halliday states that "the lexical set is identified by privilege of occurrence in collocation, just as the grammatical class is identified by privilege of occurrence in structure; the set is a grouping of items with similar tendencies of collocation."[54]

As Gleason pointed out to me, this is partly a function of the item's frequency in the text and in the reader's total language experience and any idiosyncrasy of one item that obtrudes — e.g. *phthysic* — is likely to be remembered longer (personal communication, 1968).

[53] Ferdinand de Saussure, *Course in General Linguistics* (New York, 1915), 123, 125-127.

[54] Halliday, "The Linguistic Study of Literary Texts", 304.

Such lexical items as *train, track, baggage car, rails,* constitute a lexical set, obviously incomplete, since they will regularly appear in the environment of *railroad* or *railway* and, by the same token, one member of the set will often enter into collocations with various other members of the same set.

3.7. COHESIVE FEATURES NOT STUDIED

The list of cohesive features presented in Figure 6 and in the subsequent discussion is not exhaustive. There are other linguistic phenomena which ought to be taken into account in a full study of cohesion. Modality, sequence of tenses, use of certain adjectives, comparatives, and adverbials (other than the ones mentioned in this chapter), repetition of whole clauses or parts of them, and of entire paragraphs[55] are some such features which could be added to the list in Figure 6.

In the study of cohesion in James and Hemingway which follows in Chapters 3 and 4, all cohesive features listed in Figure 6 are examined with the exception of those falling under the category of enation and agnation. The list of cohesive features studied in the subsequent chapters is, however, believed to be sufficiently inclusive to allow a meaningful examination of the cohesive relations, their patterning and their relative degrees of strength in literary prose texts.

---

[55] Cf. Alan Paton, *Cry, the Beloved Country* (New York, 1948). Lines from the first chapter of the novel are repeated at various places throughout the book. Fifteen lines of running discourse, the first paragraph and one-half of that chapter, are repeated again verbatim at the beginning of the eighteenth chapter. Again, the lines "...and the maize hardly reaches the height of a man... the men are away, the young men and the girls are away" re-occur, with slight variation, in Chapter Thirteen. The line "valleys of old men and women, of mothers and children" is repeated in the final chapter. In these examples cohesion is only part of what is accomplished.

COHESION IN JAMES

4.1. INTRODUCTION

A detailed study of cohesion in a representative passage from James' writings constitutes the main body of this chapter (sections 4.2. and 4.3.). The fourth paragraph in Chapter XLII of Henry James' *The Portrait of a Lady* has been chosen for analysis. It is a wholly narrative passage and the first shorter paragraph in that chapter. The chapter itself is considered by literary critics as characteristic of James' art and as an example of James' writing at its best. James himself describes that chapter as "obviously the best thing in the book".[1]

The text of the paragraph is examined for cohesion using the categories set up in Chapter 3. Except for the categories mentioned in section 3.7. all cohesive elements in the paragraph are described in detail. This involves some repetition but the present study of cohesion is the first of its kind and it is necessary to show explicitly what is considered cohesive and why. The discussion of cohesion in the selected paragraph exemplifies the kind of analytic work which has to be done before the tables of cohesive elements can be set up and before more general statements on the cohesiveness of a text can be made. The reader is here taken into the laboratory,

---

[1] Henry James, *The Portrait of a Lady* (New York: Random House, Modern Library College Editions, 1966), p. xli. James' comments on *The Portrait of a Lady* were made in the Preface which he wrote for the publication of the novel in the New York Edition. All quotations are from, and page references are to, the Modern Library Edition of 1966 which follows the New York Edition.

as it were, and shown exactly how the data is handled. If he wishes to see how the results presented in the tabular form later on in the chapter were arrived at he can do so by referring to the detailed description in sections 4.2. and 4.3. Each grammatical or lexical element counted as cohesive in the summary tables can be checked by referring to the description of the pair of sentences (section 4.2.) or the group of sentences (section 4.3.) in which it is found. The steps by which results are obtained are frequently — and especially in the preliminary stages of any linguistic research — equally as important as the results themselves. This justifies the detail and tediousness of the presentation in section 4.2. Another justification for presenting such a detailed description of one paragraph is that at various points in the analysis there arise several theoretical and methodological questions. As they are encountered during the analysis, these questions are dealt with, or at least marked, with the benefit of having at hand the text of the sentences which illustrate them.[2]

Section 4.2. deals with the cohesiveness of pairs of adjacent sentences and of clauses within the sentences. Any grammatical or lexical feature or item which functions as a cohesive element for two adjacent sentences or for clauses in a sentence is considered a 'tie' that joins the appropriate segments of the text. Since sentences and clauses are arranged in linear order, one following another, the second sentence in any given pair is examined for the elements which account for the connectedness of that sentence with the preceding (first) sentence.

The figures indicated at the sentence boundaries (double slashes) mark the number of cohesive elements in the sentence that follows. These elements are counted as ties between that and the preceding sentence. The number of ties for adjacent clauses is indicated at the clause boundaries (single slashes) in a similar way except that in certain cases, pointed out in the description, the figure in front of a clause may indicate the number of ties between structurally related groups of clauses rather than between two adjacent clauses.

[2] The text of the whole paragraph can be found in Appendix I. The sentences of the paragraph have been numbered for ease of reference.

A single slash (with no figure attached) marks the end of a clause which interrupts the flow of another clause.

A different method of analyzing cohesion is used in section 4.3. Here the analysis of cohesive elements goes beyond pairs of adjacent sentences. An attempt is made to show how various elements of grammatical and lexical cohesion function as ties for more than two sentences, organizing them into more or less closely related groups. The analyzed paragraph is the largest of these cohering groups of sentences.[3] Using this method of analysis it is possible to demonstrate the relationship of more than two adjacent sentences as well as of two or more sentences or groups of sentences which although not adjacent and sometimes considerably distant display the same cohesive feature or features.

A summary discussion of cohesion in the analyzed paragraph follows in section 4.4. A tabular account of the various cohesive elements is given and conclusions are drawn about the character of cohesion in the paragraph.

Portions of the text of the paragraph are quoted in the body of the chapter as illustration and reference for the description of the cohesion they display. They differ from the corresponding portions of the text in *The Portrait of a Lady* only in a few respects, all of which are graphic. Each sentence begins a new line (the original text of the paragraph is, of course, a running text) and is given a number (the parenthesized numbers) by which it is referred to in the following discussion. Sentence and clause boundaries are marked and the number of cohesive ties is indicated at these boundaries. In other respects, including the original punctuation, the text is intact.

---

[3] This is not to say that the paragraph is the largest segment of a text which can display both grammatical and lexical cohesion. There are cohesive elements in the analyzed paragraph which go beyond it in both directions, connecting this paragraph to the preceding and the following paragraph.

4.2. COHESION IN PAIRS OF ADJACENT SENTENCES AND BETWEEN CLAUSES OF INDIVIDUAL SENTENCES IN JAMES' PARAGRAPH

For ease of reference the text of each pair of sentences precedes the discussion of cohesion within that pair. The graphic arrangement and the marking of the text follow the conventions described in the introductory section of this chapter.

(1) Isabel's cheek burned /2/ when she asked herself /3/ if she had really married on a factitious theory, in order to do something finely appreciable with her money.

(2) //4// But she was able to answer quickly enough /1/ that this was only half the story.

These are the two initial sentences of the paragraph. The principal participant in the narrative is identified by name in the first clause of (1) by the phrase *Isabel's cheek*.[4] In all remaining instances in the paragraph where Isabel is mentioned directly or indirectly, this is done by the use of the third person singular feminine pronoun in either of its two forms, *she* or *her*, or through the personal possessive *her*. Since Isabel is the only feminine participant in the part of the narrative which is covered by the paragraph under discussion, there is no danger of ambiguity in assigning the correct antecedent to the anaphoric items *she* and *her*.

But functions as a coordinating connector between the two sentences. The anaphoric third person pronoun *she* of the second sentence reinforces the connection by referring to the pronoun's antecedent (Isabel) in the first sentence. The demonstrative pronoun *this* of (2) has as its antecedent the whole third clause of the first

---

[4] This is, so to speak, an oblique way of introducing the participant. It might be a question for a semantic analysis why the phrase *Isabel's cheek* is felt to be more about Isabel than her cheek. We might consider, for example, the clause *Isabel's cheek burned* as a paraphrase of *Isabel blushed*. But for our purposes it is enough to point out that in the other two clauses of (1) the personal pronoun *she* functions as subject and the pronoun's antecedent is clearly *Isabel* and not *Isabel's cheek* of the first clause.

sentence. These are three clear grammatical ties binding both sentences.

There is also one instance of lexical cohesion in the pair of sentences. The words *asked* and *answer*, in the first and second sentences respectively, form a pair of lexical items from the same co-occurrence group. *Answer* is therefore considered as a lexical item in (2) which supplies one further tie joining (2) with (1). The number of ties between (1) and (2) will now be four.

The cohesion displayed by the clauses within each of the two sentences is grammatical. Various degrees of subordination between the clauses of (1) are signalled by connectors *when* and *if*. Each of these connectors is counted as one element providing cohesion for the clauses it joins. The personal possessive *her* in the third clause is another element joining that clause with the preceding one. The connector *that* is counted as one grammatical item providing cohesion between the clauses of (2).

The grammatical items *herself* and *in order to* function each within one clause and so do not count here.

(2) But she was able to answer quickly enough / 1 / that this was only half the story.

(3) // 1 // It was / 1 / because a certain ardour took possession of her — a sense of the earnestness of his affection and a delight in his personal qualities.

The only clear instance of grammatical cohesion between (2) and (3) is due to the presence of the pronoun *her* in (3) which represents another involvement of the same participant as that marked by the pronoun *she* in (2). *Her* is therefore counted as the one item signalling grammatical cohesion between the two sentences.

It — or perhaps better the phrase *It was* — refers to the third clause of (1). Its connection with anything in (2) is only indirect, through the already established connectedness of the sentences (1) and (2). Since the connection goes beyond the pair (2)/(3) it is not marked above.

Each sentence in the pair consists of two clauses. The second clause in each sentence is marked for subordination to the first clause of that sentence. The connectors *that* and *because*, respectively in (2) and (3), mark this subordination and are counted each as one cohesive element for the pairs of clauses they join.

The presence of subordinating as well as coordinating connectors is considered part of structure and consequently connectors and the structural features they signal are not counted separately as cohesive factors. It is to be understood that every time connectors are listed in this presentation as cohesive elements, it is the grammatical structure they signal rather than their presence that is considered cohesive. Similarly, it is the various anaphoric relations that provide cohesion for the sentences and clauses in which they obtain. But for the ease of counting and referring to these relations in the text the exponents of anaphora — such as the third person personal pronouns — are indicated as the cohesive elements under the heading of grammatical cohesion.

(3) It was / 1 / because a certain ardour took possession of her — a sense of the earnestness of his affection and a delight in his personal qualities.

(4) // 1 // He was better than anyone else.

Another participant is mentioned through the two instances of the personal possessive *his* in (3) and the pronoun *he* in (4). They refer to the person of Gilbert Osmond who was mentioned by name in the preceding paragraph. *His* and *he* constitute then some of the elements that account for the cohesion of the preceding and this paragraph. *He* in (4), since it is a continuation of the same anaphoric reference as *his* in (3), is considered a cohesive factor for the two sentences also.

It should be noted that Gilbert Osmond is the only male participant in the paragraph and hence the anaphoric reference of the third person singular masculine pronoun (*he* or *him*) and of the personal possessive *his* is unambiguous throughout the paragraph, ust as the items *she* and *her* are for Isabel.

(4) He was better than anyone else.

(5) //1// This supreme conviction had filled her life for months, /3/ and enough of it still remained to prove to her /2/ that she could not have done otherwise.

Let us first consider sentence (5). It consists of three clauses joined by the coordinating connector *and* and the subordinating connector *that*. Each of the clauses contains one more cohesive element: (*her*), *her*, and *she*, respectively. The pronoun *it* in the second clause is an anaphoric substitute for the phrase *this supreme conviction* of the first clause, tying these two clauses even more strongly.

(4) is a one-clause sentence. The connection between (4) and (5) is rather complex. Generally it is achieved through the phrase *this supreme conviction* which may be seen as an anaphoric substitute for the whole sentence (4). *This*, because of its anaphoric character, is a grammatical cohesive element between (4) and (5), but *conviction*, qualified by *supreme*, although clearly cohesive cannot be classified according to the categories set up for this study. A more comprehensive treatment of cohesion would have to expand the descriptive framework to account for this kind of cohesive factor.[5]

(5) This supreme conviction had filled her life for months, /3/ and enough of it still remained to prove to her /2/ that she could not have done otherwise.

(6) //4// The finest — in the sense of being the subtlest — manly organism /2/ she had ever known / had become her property, /4/ and the recognition of her having but to put out her hands and take it had been originally a sort of act of devotion.

The first and the third clause of (6) are joined by the coordinating

---

[5] The cohesive character of the phrase *this supreme conviction* could probably be explained by establishing the equivalence of the units of the semologic stratum that are realized on the morphologic stratum by that phrase and by the whole sentence (4).

connector *and.* The second clause of (6) is embedded in the first and the connection between the two clauses is equivalent to one with the relative pronoun *that.* This feature of the zero anaphora is counted as one cohesive tie between the second and the first clause. Because of the embedding of the second clause in the first, the linear sequence of clauses in (6) is shifted, the third clause being juxtaposed directly with the first one and the second being wholly inside the first clause, attached to one phrase in that clause.

The anaphoric *it* makes another tie between the third and the first clause. Each of the three clauses of (6) contains either the pronoun *she* or one or two instances of the personal possessive *her.* These — except for the one in the first clause — serve as further cohesive elements tying the three clauses in (6).

The occurrences of the pronoun *she* and the personal possessive *her* supply the four grammatical ties between (5) and (6).

In addition to the four grammatical ties, the sentences (5) and (6) display another kind of cohesion. This cohesion is partly lexical, but as in (4)/(5) this type of cohesion should probably be stated in different terms. *The finest... manly organism* is somehow related to *this supreme conviction* of (5) which in turn refers to the whole sentence (4): *he was better than anyone else.* However, since this kind of cohesion is outside the categories of cohesive factors set up in Chapter 2 it is not counted as a tie between (5) and (6).

> (6) The finest — in the sense of being the subtlest — manly organism /2/ she had ever known / had become her property, /4/ and the recognition of her having but to put out her hands and take it had been originally a sort of act of devotion.
>
> (7) //2// She had not been mistaken about the beauty of his mind; /3/ she knew that organ perfectly now.

The two occurrences of the pronoun *she* in (7) supply the ties between that and the preceding sentence. In some more comprehensive framework of the study of cohesion *his* might be also considered a cohesive factor for the pair of sentences. Within the framework of the present analysis, however, *his* of (7) can be seen as cohesive only in relation to sentence (4).

Sentence (7) contains two independent clauses which are loosely coordinated through the semicolon. This rather loose coordination, which is dependent on the punctuation, is not counted as one of the cohesive elements in (7) since punctuation is not treated in the present analysis. The three ties between the clauses are due to the pronoun *she* and the phrase *that organ* in the second clause. The latter is two-fold cohesive. The demonstrative *that* functions as a grammatical cohesive element through its anaphoric reference to the phrase *his mind*, while the word *organ* provides lexical cohesion since it is — at least in (7) — a synonym for *mind*.

(7) She had not been mistaken about the beauty of his mind; /3/ she knew that organ perfectly now.

(8) //6// She had lived with it, /3/ she had lived *in* it almost — /3/ it appeared to have become her habitation.

The connectedness of (7) and (8) is displayed six times through the instances of *she, her,* and *it,* the pronoun *it* in (8) having for its antecedents both *his mind* and *that organ* in (7). The same elements account for the grammatical cohesion between the clauses of (8). The repetition of the lexical item *lived* (in both cases *lived* is part of the phrase *she had lived*) provides lexical cohesion between the first two clauses. *Habitation* is a lexical item in the third clause cohering with *lived in* of the second clause.

(8) She had lived with it, /3/ she had lived *in* it almost — /3/ it appeared to have become her habitation.

(9) //3// If she had been captured /2/ it had taken a firm hand to seize her; /1/ that reflection perhaps had some worth.

She, it, and *her* in (9) are the cohesive elements connecting this sentence with (8). The second clause of (8) is connected to the first one in two ways — structurally, through the subordinating connector *if,* and anaphorically, through the personal possessive *her*. The third clause displays cohesion not so much with the second clause as with both the first and the second clause since the two form a structural unit. The determiner *that* of the phrase *that reflection* is anaphoric since the phrase refers to the statement contained in the first two clauses of (9).

(9) If she had been captured /2/ it had taken a firm hand to seize her; /1/ that reflection perhaps had some worth.
(10) //5// A mind more ingenious, more pliant, more cultivated, more trained to admirable exercises, she had not encountered; /4/ and it was this exquisite instrument /1/ she had now to reckon with.

The cohesion of (9) and (10) is both grammatical and lexical. The lexical items *mind* and *instrument* in (10) refer to the same thing as does the pronoun *it* in (9) since *it* in turn is an anaphoric substitute for the earlier *mind* and *organ* of (7). As elements of lexical cohesion, *mind* and *instrument* therefore work across a larger portion of the text, their synonyms being found in an earlier sentence with two sentences coming in between. The latter two sentences, however, contain the anaphoric *it* which constitutes a link between the two sets of synonyms. *Mind* is the stronger lexical cohesive element of the two since it is a repetition of the same word. An intricate network of cohesive relations emerges when a larger portion of the text is considered. But for the moment I want only to mark these relations as they are touched upon in the analysis of separate pairs of adjacent sentences. A more comprehensive discussion of cohesion in the paragraph will follow later.

The noun phrase which is headed by the noun *instrument* contains the determiner *this* which, itself a factor of grammatical cohesion, reinforces the lexical cohesion. The two occurrences of the pronoun *she* bring the number of cohesive elements up to five — three grammatical and two lexical ones.

The second and the third clauses of (10) form a unit with the feature of the zero anaphora (in place of the relative *that*) providing the one tie. Both clauses as a unit are joined with the first clause by the coordinating connector *and*. The pronoun *she* is another cohesive factor. Two more cohesive elements are contained in the phrase *this exquisite instrument*, functioning in very much the same way for the two clauses as they do for the two sentences. The phrase is, of course, an anaphoric substitute for the noun *mind* of the first clause. The number of cohesive elements for the pair of clauses, that is, for the first clause and the second together with the third, will then be four — three grammatical and one lexical.

(10) A mind more ingenious, more pliant, more cultivated, more trained to admirable exercises, she had not encountered; /4/ and it was this exquisite instrument /1/ she had now to reckon with.

(11) //2// She lost herself in infinite dismay /2/ when she thought of the magnitude of his deception.

There are two grammatical ties between (10) and (11), both due to the two occurrences of the pronoun *she* in (11). The reflexive pronoun *herself*, while a cohesive element within the first clause of (11), is not considered an extra tie between the two sentences since the reflexive pronouns are restricted in their cohesive function to single clauses.

The two clauses of (11) display two ties — one due to the connector *when* and the other to the pronoun *she*. The personal possessive *his*, although not counted for the pair (10)/(11), is a cohesive element functioning across a number of preceding sentences.

(11) She lost herself in infinite dismay /2/ when she thought of the magnitude of his deception.

(12) //3// It was a wonder, perhaps, in view of this, /1/ that he didn't hate her more.

The sentences (11) and (12) display three ties. The demonstrative pronoun *this* in (12) has an anaphoric function since it refers to the phrase *the magnitude of his deception* in (11). The personal pronoun *he* in (12) and the personal possessive *his* in (11) refer to the same person — Gilbert Osmond. *She,* twice in (11), and *her* in (12) provide still another tie for the pair of sentences. The connector *that* is the only cohesive element between the clauses of the second sentence.

(12) It was a wonder, perhaps, in view of this, /1/ that he didn't hate her more.

(13) //5// She remembered perfectly the first sign /1/ he had given of it — /1/ it had been like the bell /2/ that was to ring up the curtain upon the real drama of their life.

The cohesion of the two sentences is wholly grammatical, similar to that in the preceding pair and in many other pairs of adjacent sentences in the paragraph. It is due to the occurrence of the pronouns *she* and *he* in (13) and of the personal possessive *their* which refers jointly to the two participants in the narrative. The pronoun *it* in the second clause of (13) appears to be an anaphoric substitute for the idea expressed in (12) and also in (11). While it is difficult to state exactly what this *it* replaces it is obvious that *it* refers to what has been said in (12) and in (11) as well. The function of *it* is therefore anaphoric and the pronoun has to be counted as another cohesive element in the pair. The grammatical character of the pronoun *it* in the third clause is more ambiguous. But since one of its functions can be interpreted similarly to that of the first *it* the pronoun is also considered cohesive.

The difficulty of stating the exact antecedent for *it* of the second clause of (13) indicates again that some other more comprehensive framework of description is needed for a more thorough and rigorous statement of the problem of cohesion. Nevertheless, the present analysis using the categories set up in Chapter 3, while not always allowing a precise statement, illustrates fairly adequately the problem of cohesion and is therefore useful as a way of breaking into some aspects of the discourse analysis of literary texts.

There are four clauses in (13). The first and second clauses form a structural unit. The one tie indicated between them refers to the feature of the zero anaphora on which the cohesion of both clauses depends. The connection between the first together with the second clause and the third clause is established through the pronoun *it* of the third clause. The dash strengthens the connection but is not counted here as a cohesive element since punctuation is not treated.

The connection between the third and the fourth clause of (13) is structural again. *That* of the fourth clause marks this connection. This *that* is different from *that* in (12). The latter functions as a connector only, signalling the structure of subordination. *That* in (13) is not only a connector introducing the subordinate fourth clause but it also performs the grammatical function of the subject of the fourth clause. The way *that* of (13) functions as a connector is also different from the way *that* of (12) does. *That* of (13), which is the first element of the subordinate clause, functions as an anaphoric substitute for *the bell*, the last element of the main clause. The nature of the tie provided by *that* of (13) is then more complex and, it is suggested, more cohesive than that of the graphically identical word in (12). All this proves the point made in the third chapter that in English different connectors — and sometimes those apparently the same — indicate various degrees of subordination or coordination and that they may differ in their cohesive strength. This also raises the question of the relative value of particular cohesive ties.[6]

One more cohesive factor has to be mentioned while analyzing the connectedness of the two last clauses of (13). These clauses also display lexical cohesion through the pair *bell* and *ring up*, two items of same co-occurrence group. The cohesion between these two clauses is then both grammatical and lexical, each kind providing one tie.

(13) She remembered perfectly the first sign / 1 / he had given of

---

[6] While marking the problem of the differentiation in the degree of cohesiveness that various connectors provide, I am not attempting to represent this fact numerically at the points where the number of cohesive ties is indicated. To do this it would be necessary to devise a system for evaluating the relative strength of connectedness between sentences and especially clauses. This would require a separate study.

it — /1/ it had been like the bell /2/ that was to ring up the curtain upon the real drama of their life.

(14) //4// He said to her one day /2/ that she had too many ideas /4/ and that she must get rid of them.

The cohesion of (13) and (14) is again grammatical. *He, her,* and *she* (occurring twice) make up the cohesive elements in this pair of sentences.

The second sentence consists of three clauses, the second and the third joined by the coordinating connector *and.* The pronouns *she* and *them* of the third clause constitute two more cohesive elements between that and the second clause. *Them* has *ideas* for its antecedent. The repetition in the third clause of the same connector (and clause introducer) as in the second is regarded as still another tie between these clauses.

Besides being coordinated with each other both the second and third clauses are subordinated to the first clause. The second and the third clause each contain the subordinating connector *that* and the pronoun *she* which supply the two ties between these and the first clause.

It also is possible to view the three clauses of (14) as forming a network of interrelations rather than a chain of concatenated units. From this point of view the two subordinate clauses are related to the main clause not only as a unit of two coordinated clauses but also as two individual units since each is introduced by a separate connector. Two cohesive elements of the third clause would then have to be counted twice.

(14) He said to her one day /2/ that she had too many ideas /4/ and that she must get rid of them.

(15) //9// He had told her that already, before their marriage; /4/ but then she had not noticed it: /3/ it had come back to her only afterwards.

The above pair of sentences displays strong cohesion. In addition to the four occurrences of the third person singular pronouns (*he, her, she,* and *her* again) there is the personal possessive *their.* The demonstrative pronoun *that* in (15) refers clearly to the content of the second and third clauses of (14) and so does *it* which occurs twice. The phrase *told her* in (15) is repetitious in relation to the synonymous phrase *said to her* in (14) and, therefore, *told* and *said* can be seen as an instance of lexical cohesion.[7] Altogether there are nine elements constituting cohesion of the two sentences; eight are grammatical and only one is lexical.

Each of the three clauses of (15) contain a temporal adverb or phrase. The latter are related in pairs. These pairs of temporals function as cohesive ties between the clauses in which they are found. The second clause has the adverb *then* which refers to the same time in the past as does the phrase *before their marriage* in the first clause. *Afterwards* of the third clause may be considered one of the pair of temporals with either *then* or *before their marriage.*

The connector *but* and the pronouns *she* and *it* make three more ties between the first and second clauses. Similarly the pronouns *it* and *her* of the third clause provide further ties joining that clause and the preceding one.

The connections between clauses in (15) unlike those in (14) represent a linear arrangement with clauses concatenated and forming a chain, not a tree.

(15) He had told her that already, before their marriage; /4/ but then she had not noticed it: /3/ it had come back to her only afterwards.

(16) //6// This time she might well have noticed it, /2/ because he had really meant it.

---

[7] The verbs *say* and *tell* are frequent lexical items and as such would not be normally counted as elements of lexical cohesion. But in (14)/(15) they are found in parallel constructions, with identical subjects and objects, and this fact makes them cohesive for the pair of sentences. Structural parallelism by itself is not counted as a cohesive element in the present study because too little is known about it to make any count of this feature meaningful. Parallel structures will be indicated, however, in those cases where they result in endowing lexical or grammatical items with cohesive properties — as in the pair of sentences under discussion.

One of the ties between (15) and (16) is due to the adverbial phrase *this time* at the beginning of the second sentence. The phrase is related to both the adverb *afterwards* and the adverb *then* of (15) with which it forms a pair of temporals. *She*, *he*, and the two occurrences of *it* make four more ties in the manner described above. There is a repetition of the verb *notice* which by itself would not be a strong argument for lexical cohesion of the two sentences since this word is a fairly frequent lexical item. However, as with *say* and *tell* in (14)/(15) the strong structural parallelism of the clauses in which the verb functions — including the identity of the subjects and of the objects — justifies the consideration of the two occurrences of *notice* as another cohesive factor.

The above passage is another instance of a pair of strongly cohesive sentences. Most of the cohesive elements are grammatical (six) and one only is lexical. Even this one item of lexical cohesion is partly due to grammatical structure.

There are two ties between the second and first clauses of (16): the connector *because* and the pronoun *it*.

(16) This time she might well have noticed it, /2/ because he had really meant it.

(17) //2// The words had been nothing superficially; /3/ but when in the light of deepening experience she had looked into them /2/ they had then appeared portentous.

Two grammatical ties join (16) and (17): the pronoun *she* and the determiner *the*. The anaphoric character of the latter is determined by the fact that the head of the noun phrase of which *the* is part refers to the words spoken by Gilbert Osmond. Although these words are not to be found in the preceding sentence but in an earlier one, the content of these words is referred to anaphorically in (16) by the pronoun *it*.

The second and third clauses contain the pair of temporals *when... then*, which bind them structurally, and the pronouns *them/they* in the second and the third clause respectively, which have the same antecedent — *the words* of the first clause. Both pronouns function also as cohesive ties between the last two clauses and the third clause of (17). *But* serves as a connector for these clauses.

(17) The words had been nothing superficially; /3/ but when in the light of deepening experience she had looked into them /2/ they had then appeared portentous.

(18) //4// He had really meant it — /1/ he would have liked her to have nothing of her own but her pretty appearance.

The personal pronoun *her* together with the two instances of *her* as a personal possessive make three clear grammatical ties between (17) and (18). With the fourth tie, the pronoun *it*, the situation is somewhat less obvious. It is anaphoric and appears to refer in some way to the phrase *the words* in (17) since the latter refers in turn to the opinion expressed by Osmond in an earlier sentence — that Isabel had too many ideas and would have to get rid of them. Because of that *it* is counted as a cohesive factor for the pair of sentences, although it is possible to argue against this decision. We have here still another instance of the kind of cohesion the examination of which calls for a more comprehensive framework of description.

The pronoun *he* is the only grammatical tie between the two clauses of (18).

(18) He had really meant it — /1/ he would have liked her to have nothing of her own but her pretty appearance.

(19) //9// She had known /2/ she had too many ideas; /1/ she had more even /1/ than he had supposed, /3/ many more than she had expressed to him /4/ when he had asked her to marry him.

All nine ties between (18) and (19) are due to the occurrences of the personal pronouns *she, her, he,* and *him* in (19). As was pointed out in the discussion of (17)/(18) the anaphoric reference of the pronoun *it* of (18) is to Osmond's opinion that Isabel "had too many ideas and that she must get rid of them". But that opinion was expressed in an earlier sentence, removed from (18) by four intervening sentences. Each of these four sentences contains an anaphoric element referring to that opinion (*that, it, the words, they*). We could consider the whole clause *she had too many ideas* of (19) as another cohesive element in (18)/(19) if it were not for the fact that the pronoun *it* of (18), being so far removed from its original antecedent, begins to be less transparent in regard to its anaphoric function. The cohesive link between (18) and (19) due to the relation of the second clause of (19) to the pronoun *it* of (18) is therefore not so obvious and is not counted as a tie between these sentences. It may be remarked, however, that the clause *she had too many ideas* functions as a strong cohesive element between sentence (19) and the earlier sentence (14) which contains the same clause.

The division of (19) into clauses may appear arbitrary at one or two points (at the third and fourth clause boundaries). A certain degree of arbitrariness is, however, unavoidable in this kind of linguistic analysis. The six clauses of (19) form three pairs of structurally closely related ones — the first with the second, the third with the fourth, and the fifth with the sixth clause. These three pairs are in turn connected with one another, the preceding with the following clause (linear order of connections), but not so closely as the clauses within the pairs.

The third and fifth clauses contain respectively the items *more* and *many more*. The examination of the cohesive function of *more* in (19) leads to assigning it a double character. In one respect it is a grammatical substitute for the phrase (*too*) *many ideas* of the second clause. *More* also affects the meaning of the phrase for which it substitutes. While the latter function of *more* may or may not be considered cohesive (lexical cohesion), the former function has to be regarded as such and, consequently, *more* is being counted as one element of grammatical cohesion for the clauses it joins.

The boundary between the third and fourth clauses separates two items, *even* and *than*, which function as two elements of one connector. *Than* by itself would be sufficient to establish the connection between the clauses. The presence of *even* in the preceding clause anticipates the presence of *than* in the following clause and thus strengthens the connective function of *than*. *Even* is shown to belong to the third clause since that clause appears to be a stylistic variation of *she had even more*. But this is, as noted above, an arbitrary decision.

The phrase *many more* at the beginning of the fifth clause is partly a repetition of an element of the third clause and as such it is counted as one tie between the fifth and the third and fourth clauses.

The other cohesive elements in the adjacent clauses and pairs of clauses are the pronouns *she, her, he,* and *him,* together with the connectors *than* and *when.*

(19) She had known /2/ she had too many ideas; /1/ she had more even /1/ than he had supposed, /3/ many more than she had expressed to him /4/ when he had asked her to marry him.

(20) //3// Yes, she *had* been hypocritical; /1/ she had liked him so much.

The three ties between (19) and (20) are grammatical, pronouns supplying them. The above two sentences are cohesive also in another way. The clause in (20) describing Isabel as *hypocritical* is semantically closely related to the whole sentence (19). This kind of cohesion is, however, beyond the scope of the present study.

The division of (20) into clauses is again somewhat arbitrary. *Yes* is not set apart as a separate unit because there is no category in the framework of this description that would justify a different treatment of this item. An examination of cohesion which would also include a semantic discussion of the text might consider *yes* separately from the two clauses. *She* provides the one tie between the clauses in (20).

(20) Yes, she *had* been hypocritical; / 1 / she had liked him so much.

(21) // 1 // She had too many ideas for herself; / 3 / but that was just / Ø / what one married for, / to share them with some one else.

The pronoun *she*, reinforced by *herself*, is the only cohesive element between (20) and (21). The cohesion within sentence (21), however, is rather intricate as will be seen below.

The division of (21) into clauses poses some problems.[8] It has been segmented into three clauses with the second clause reading *but that was just... to share them with some one else* — the dots marking the position of the third embedded clause. As is suggested in footnote 8 of this chapter, *that* functions as a place holder for the phrase *to share them with some one else*. An alternative version of the second and third clauses would then read *but to share them with some one else was just what one married for*. James' version may be seen as a stylistic variation. It is the better version of the two from the point of view of cohesion. Both versions contain the pronoun *them* which supplies one cohesive element through its function as an anaphoric substitute for *ideas* of the first clause. But James' version contains, moreover, the pronoun *that* which functions both as an anaphoric and cataphoric demonstrative. In its anaphoric function *that* refers to the whole first clause and thus supplies an extra tie between that and the second and third clauses. Its simultaneous cataphoric function, as an anticipatory place holder for a later phrase which is separated from the rest of its clause by another clause, accounts for the internal cohesion of the second clause.

[8]   The text of (21) between the semicolon and the period is considered to consist of two clauses, the second clause *what one married for* being embedded in the first. It is suggested that the two clauses are a result of applying transformations to some structurally simpler underlying sentences. For the purposes of description of cohesion in (21) it is not necessary to present the whole derivation. It suffices to show the last stage of that derivation which would be the applying of a transformation to the sentence "but to share them with some one else was just what one married for." The transformation replaces the subject in the suggested sentence with the anticipatory *that*, moving the original subject to the end position in the sentence and giving the sentence the form found in (21).

The connection between the second and the third clauses of (21) is not indicated by connectors or anaphoric items and consequently no tie is indicated between the two clauses. The second and the third clause are joined with the first by the connector *but*, the demonstrative pronoun *that* in its anaphoric function, and the pronoun *them* whose antecedent is the word *ideas* of the first clause.

(21) She had too many ideas for herself; /3/ but that was just /∅/ what one married for, / to share them with some one else.

(22) //3// One couldn't pluck them up by the roots, /2/ though of course one might suppress them, /1/ be careful not to utter them.

The three ties between (21) and (22) are provided by the three occurrences of the pronoun *them*. It might also be argued that the two occurrences of the indefinite pronoun *one* in (22) should be considered cohesive because of the similar use of *one* in (21). But since this question cannot be solved without referring to the semologic structure they are not counted as cohesive for (21)/(22).

The connector *though* and the pronoun *them* serve as ties between the first and second clauses of (22). *Them* also provides one tie for the second and third clauses of that sentence.

(22) One couldn't pluck them up by the roots, /2/ though of course one might suppress them, /1/ be careful not to utter them.

(23) //∅// It had not been this, however, his objecting to her opinions; /1/ this had been nothing.

All pairs of adjacent sentences so far have had anaphoric items — usually personal pronouns or personal possessives, as some or all cohesive elements. There are no such elements in (22). The only candidate for a grammatical cohesive element, the coordinating connector *however*, does not appear to join (22) and (23) directly.

Rather it joins (22) with a whole group of the preceding sentences. The function of the connector cannot be explained within the pair of the adjacent sentences and it will be discussed in section 4.3. There are no lexical cohesive elements in (22)/(23). The number of cohesive ties for the pair will then be Ø. This is the only instance in the analyzed paragraph where not a single item belonging to the cohesive categories dealt with in this study can be shown to tie two adjacent sentences.

This of the first clause of (23) is both anaphoric and cataphoric. The pronoun is removed from its antecedent by many intervening sentences. It might not be quite clear what the pronoun *this* refers to if it were not followed by a restatement of its antecedent. The latter is, so to speak, planted later on in the same clause where *this* is found through the phrase *his objecting to her opinions*. In relation to that phrase the pronoun *this* is cataphoric. We have here again an instance of a demonstrative pronoun which is both anaphoric and cataphoric. This use of demonstrative pronouns appears to be a device employed by James to ensure that his pronouns always have clear antecedents. Since so much of the cohesion in the text analyzed depends on pronouns the importance of their clear reference is apparent.

The second *this* of (23) is wholly anaphoric and supplies the one tie between the two clauses. It is a very strong tie since the pronoun follows its antecedent immediately.

(23) It had not been this, however, his objecting to her opinions; /1/ this had been nothing.

(24) //3// She had no opinions — /3/ none that she would not have been eager to sacrifice in the satisfaction of feeling herself loved for it.

The cohesion between (23) and (24) is both grammatical and lexical. Two grammatical ties are due to the occurrences of the pronoun *she* in (24) and one lexical tie is supplied by the word *opinions*. *None* is not considered a grammatical tie between the two sentences although it functions as such for the clauses in (24).

The pronoun *none* is an example of the category of cohesive items listed under the heading of "nominal substitutes" in the third chapter. In (24) *none* functions as a link between its two clauses. It substitutes for the phrase *no opinions*, functioning as a cohesive link in conjunction with another cohesive item, the relative pronoun *that*. The pronoun *she* of the second clause makes the third tie.

(24) She had no opinions — /3/ none that she would not have been eager to sacrifice in the satisfaction of feeling herself loved for it.

(25) //3// What he had meant /Ø/ had been the whole thing — her character, /Ø/ the way she felt, /2/ the way she judged.

The personal possessive *her* and the pronoun *she* supply the cohesive elements in (24)/(25).

Only the third and the fourth clause of (25) contain cohesive elements which are studied here. These are the pronoun *she* and the lexical item *way* repeated in parallel constructions.

(25) What he had meant /Ø/ had been the whole thing — her character, /Ø/ the way she felt, /2/ the way she judged.

(26) //6// This was /Ø/ what she had kept in reserve; /1/ this was /Ø/ what he had not known /3/ until he had found himself — /Ø/ with the door closed behind, as it were — / set down face to face with it.

The demonstrative pronoun *this*, occurring twice in (26), has for its antecedent what is expressed by the second, third, and fourth clauses of (25). The occurrences of *she* and *he* provide three more cohesive elements in (25)/(26). The second *it*, having the same antecedent as *this*, provides the sixth tie.

The only justification for treating (26) as one sentence rather than two is the fact that James used a semicolon instead of a period at the end of the second clause. Punctuation, however, although not studied here is an important factor in the consideration of cohesion in a written text and this analysis proceeds on the assumption that anything contained between two periods is meant to be one sentence.

The first and the second clause of (26) are related structurally, as are the third and the fourth clauses. But since there are no connectors nor anaphoric items functioning in the two pairs of clauses, no ties are indicated at the respective clause boundaries. *This* of the third clause functions as the one cohesive tie between the two pairs of structurally related clauses. The fifth clause is joined to the third and fourth clauses by the temporal connector *until* and the anaphoric *he* and *it*. The latter refers to the demonstrative pronoun *this*. The flow of the fifth clause is interrupted by a parenthesis indicated by a pair of dashes. The parenthesis is only tenuously connected with the fifth clause, dashes indicating this connection. Since punctuation is not treated here the connection has been marked as zero ('Ø').

(26) This was /Ø/ what she had kept in reserve; /1/ this was /Ø/ what he had not known /3/ until he had found himself — /Ø/ with the door closed behind, as it were — / set down face to face with it.

(27) //2// She had a certain way of looking at life /1/ which he took as a personal offence.

The pronouns *she* and *he* supply the cohesive ties between (26) and (27). The two clauses of (27) are joined by one tie, the relative pronoun *which*.

(27) She had a certain way of looking at life /1/ which he took as a personal offence.

(28) //2// Heaven knew /1/ that now at least it was a very humble, accommodating way!

There are two elements in (28) which function as ties between that sentence and (27). Both elements refer to the phrase *a certain way of looking at life* in the first sentence. They are the anaphoric *it* and the lexical item *way* in (28) since the construction in which this second *way* is found indicates that it is identical with the first *way*. That construction is of an equative type — the pronoun *it* is equated with the phrase *a very humble, accommodating way*. *It* is in turn anaphoric in relation to the phrase in (27) containing the first *way*. This identical character of *way* in both instances must be pointed out because otherwise the lexical item *way*, which is relatively frequent in English, could not be considered a cohesive factor. The repetition of *way* provides one tie of lexical cohesion, the other tie (*it*) being grammatical.

The cohesion between the clauses of (28) is structural, the subordinating connector *that* marking it.

(28) Heaven knew /1/ that now at least it was a very humble, accommodating way!

(29) //1// The strange thing was /1/ that she should not have suspected from the first /1/ that his own had been so different.

The phrase *his own* is the only tie — if any — between (28) and (29). That phrase presents some problems as to how it functions in its anaphoric character. It may be maintained that either *his* by itself or the whole phrase *his own* is an element of nominal substitution replacing the phrase *way of looking at life* of (27) and thus simultaneously being related to the phrase containing the lexical item *way* in (28). These are, though, two different 'ways of looking at life', as they are ascribed to two different people. Some semantic questions are involved here which are beyond the scope of this presentation. Nevertheless, the phrase *his own* has been counted as a grammatical cohesive element because at least one of its functions is grammatical substitution for an element that is partly present in the preceding sentence.

There is one cohesive element for each pair of adjacent clauses in (29). In both cases that element is the structural feature of subordination marked by the connector *that*.

(29) The strange thing was / 1 / that she should not have suspected from the first / 1 / that his own had been so different.

(30) // 3 // She had thought it so large, so enlightened, so perfectly that of an honest man and a gentleman.

One of the three ties between (29) and (30) is the pronoun *she* and needs no further description. The second tie depends on the anaphoric function of the pronoun *it* of (30). That pronoun refers to the same concept for which the phrase *his own* of (29) substitutes. While this *it* is obviously anaphoric and related to *his own*, and as such counted as a cohesive factor for the pair of sentences, there arise some semantic questions concerning the pronoun's antecedent similar to those mentioned in the discussion of (28)/(29). The anaphoric *that* is the third tie — its reference being the same as in the case of *it*.

(30) She had thought it so large, so enlightened, so perfectly that of an honest man and a gentleman.

(31) // 1 // Hadn't he assured her / 2 / that he had no superstitions, no dull limitations, no prejudices / 2 / that had lost their freshness?

The personal pronoun *her* of (31) makes the only tie between that sentence and (30). The two ties between the first and second clauses of (31) are grammatical — *that*, marking subordination, and the pronoun *he* of the second clause. There are also two items of grammatical cohesion for the second and third clauses. They are the relative pronoun *that* and the personal possessive *their*.

(31) Hadn't he assured her / 2 / that he had no superstitions, no dull limitations, no prejudices / 2 / that had lost their freshness?

(32) // 1 // Hadn't he all the appearance of a man living in the open air of the world, indifferent to small considerations, caring only for truth and knowledge and believing / 2 / that two intelligent people ought to look for them together and,

/3/ whether they found them or not, / find at last some happiness in the search?

Parallel constructions are not treated in this study unless they reinforce lexical cohesion. Accordingly only the pronoun *he* is counted as a cohesive factor for (31)/(32).

The pronoun *them* in the second clause of (32) supplies one grammatical tie between that clause and the preceding one in which its antecedent, the phrase *truth and knowledge,* is found. The other tie is marked by *that.* The third clause interrupts the flow of the second clause and can be seen as a parenthetical statement. It is, however, more closely related to the clause it interrupts than parentheses generally are. The third parenthetical clause is joined to the second clause by three ties — the connector *whether* and the pronouns *they* and *them.* Each of the two pronouns has a different antecedent. *They* refers to the phrase *two intelligent people* while *them* replaces the phrase *truth and knowledge.* No ambiguity can arise while assigning these antecedents to their pronouns since the phrase *two intelligent people,* which functions as the subject of the second clause, can be replaced only by the pronoun *they* and not its objective form *them.*

(32) Hadn't he all the appearance of a man living in the open air of the world, indifferent to small considerations, caring only for truth and knowledge and believing /2/ that two intelligent people ought to look for them together and, /3/ whether they found them or not, / find at last some happiness in the search?

(33) //2// He had told her /1/ he loved the conventional; /2/ but there was a sense /1/ in which this seemed a noble declaration.

The two ties between (32) and (33) are supplied by the two occurrences of the pronoun *he* in (33).

The pronoun *he* of the second clause of (33) provides the one tie between that and the first clause. The third and the fourth clause are best seen as jointly connected to the preceding ones by the coordinating connector *but*. The anaphoric *this* is the other cohesive element between the two pairs of clauses. The relative *which* in the fourth clause marks the subordination of that clause to the third and is counted as one tie between them.

(33) He had told her /1/ he loved the conventional; /2/ but there was a sense /1/ in which this seemed a noble declaration.

(34) //5// In that sense, that of the love of harmony and order and decency and of all the stately offices of life, she went with him freely, /2/ and his warning had contained nothing ominous.

The first *that* in (34), the determiner in the noun phrase *that sense*, is both anaphoric and cataphoric. In its anaphoric function it supplies the first tie between (33) and (34). The head of the noun phrase can be seen as a lexical cohesive item since the anaphoric *that* marks the noun *sense* in (34) as identical with the same noun in (33). The other three ties in the two adjacent sentences (33)/(34) are due to the occurrences of *she, him,* and *his* in (34).

It may be noted that the second *that* in (34) serves as a cohesive element only within the first clause of that sentence. The coordinating connector *and* and the personal possessive *his* are the two ties between the first and second clauses of (34).

(34) In that sense, that of the love of harmony and order and decency and of all the stately offices of life, she went with him freely, /2/ and his warning had contained nothing ominous.

(35) //8// But when, /1/ as months had elapsed, / she had followed him further /4/ and he had led her into the mansion of his own habitation, /3/ then, *then* she had seen /2/ where she really was.

All eight ties between (34) and (35) are grammatical. Six of them are due to the occurrences of the third person pronouns *he* and *she* in either of their two forms. One is the personal possessive *his* and one other, which comes first in order, is the connector *but*. The other connector *when*, which follows *but* immediately, does not function as a cohesive element for the two sentences.

There are five clauses in (35). The second clause, which interrupts the flow of the first clause immediately after its first element, is joined to the first clause by the subordinating connector *as*. The coordinating connector *and* together with the pronouns *he* and *her* and the personal possessive *his* make the four ties between the first and the third clauses (which are adjacent, as the second clause is inserted in the first). The fourth and fifth clauses have two ties, *where* and *she*. The pair of temporals *when... then*, with the second *then* for emphasis, indicate a more complex interrelationship of clauses in (35) than simply the connection of the adjacent ones. The pair of temporals marks two groups of clauses which it also connects structurally — the first three and the remaining two clauses. The figure 'three' in front of the fourth clause is to be interpreted therefore as the number of ties between the two groups of clauses. Besides the connection through the pair of temporals there are also two further ties due to the occurrences of the pronoun *she* in the second group.

4.3. OVERALL COHESION IN THE PARAGRAPH

4.3.1. Method

In section 4.2. the examination of cohesion in the paragraph studied was limited to pairs of adjacent sentences. All cohesive elements and their function as ties between these pairs of sentences were described separately for each pair. The whole paragraph can be seen according to that description as a chain of adjacent sentences, each joined with the sentence that precedes it.

A different method of examining cohesion is used in this section. Cohesive elements are studied individually in relation to the whole paragraph or that portion of it in which they function.

A different picture of cohesion emerges when this approach is taken. Various overlapping patterns of cohesive relations show connectedness not only between adjacent sentences but also among whole groups of sentences, whether adjacent or not. The largest of these groups includes all the sentences in the paragraph studied.

4.3.2. Grammatical cohesion: anaphora

It is apparent from the discussion in section 4.2. that a large majority of the cohesive elements functioning as ties for adjacent sentences are grammatical and that the items subsumed under the heading of anaphora provide most of the grammatical ties between sentences. The following description begins therefore with the examination of anaphora. Table 1 gives a graphic representation of the over-all distribution of the anaphoric items and their cohesive function in the paragraph. Since sentence is used as a unit in the table, anaphoric items which function within one sentence only are not indicated.

Here are some explanations for the notation used in Table 1.

x	antecedent present in the sentence.
*	anaphoric item or items of the kind represented in a given column present in the sentence.
x—*	both the anaphoric item and the restated antecedent present in the sentence.
*—x	the anaphoric item is also cataphoric because its antecedent is repeated later on in the same sentence.
——	(solid line) connects items with the same anaphoric reference in the same or adjacent sentences.
- - -	(dotted line) connects such items in non-adjacent sentences.
═══	(double line) indicates that antecedent is the same for the different anaphoric items.
(column) 1	the third person personal pronouns and personal possessives which mark the involvement of the two participants in the narrative:

(a) *she* and *her*, referring to *Isabel*,

(b) *their*, referring to both *Isabel* and *Osmond*,

(c) *he*, *him*, and *his*, referring to *Osmond*.

(column) 2 personal pronouns with different antecedents:

(a) *it*,

(b) *them*.

(column) 3 demonstrative pronouns (different antecedents):

(a) *this*,

(b) *that*.

(column) 4 determiners (different antecedents):

(a) *the*,

(b) *this*,

(c) *that*.

(column) 5 substitutes.

(column) 6 adverbs.

The representation of anaphora in Table 1 indicates that the anaphoric items found in the sentences of James' paragraph fall into two groups — those whose anaphoric reference remains unchanged throughout the paragraph and those which have different antecedents in different parts of the paragraph.

The personal pronouns in column 1 belong to the first group since their antecedents remain unchanged. Every time an item from this group appears in the text it marks an involvement of one of the two participants in the narrative: the pronouns *she*, *her*, and the possessive *her* referring always to Isabel and the forms *he*, *him*, and *his* referring to Osmond. *Their* marks a joint involvement of Isabel and Osmond. The occurrences of the personal pronouns in column 1 can be seen as forming two lines of participant involvement. Although there are some gaps in these lines they seem to provide a backbone for the cohesion of the whole paragraph, with the other cohesive elements reinforcing that cohesion by supplying additional connectedness for various smaller groups of sentences.

The pronouns in 1a and 1c are the only anaphoric elements which function in larger groups of adjacent sentences. The largest of these groups consists of seventeen sentences, (5)-(21), due to the

TABLE 1

Anaphora in James' paragraph

continuous presence of *she/her*. There are only four separate sentences in which no *she/her* items occur. We have therefore five groups of adjacent sentences which are cohesive due to the anaphoric items in 1a. These groups are also cohesive in relation to one another for the same reason.

The groups of sentences which are cohesive due to the anaphoric items in 1c include a smaller number of sentences. They represent a chain of cohesive sentences parallel to that in 1a. At two points both chains are joined through the common anaphoric element *their* of 1b. We speak of two chains of sentences not because they are different sentences (in most cases they are not) but because they represent two ways of grouping the sentences of the paragraph. The gap in 1a at sentence (32) is bridged wholly and the gap at sentence (4) partially because of the cohesiveness of the sentences adjacent to (4) and (32) due to the anaphoric items in 1c.

The mutually reinforcing character of cohesive items in 1a, 1b, and 1c is apparent from the table. Considering the cohesive function of these items only, three groups of related sentences can be turned out: (1)-(21), (23)-(27), and (29)-(35), with sentences (22) and (28) as gaps in this sequence. The latter two sentences are gaps in the sequence of consecutive sentences only in regard to the cohesive items listed in column 1. They cohere with the sentences immediately preceding and following them due to the presence of other cohesive factors (cf. columns 2, 3, and 4). Sentence (23) is the only one which does not contain any anaphoric or other grammatical or lexical item to provide cohesion with the immediately preceding sentence.

A few observations can be made about the cohesive character of the anaphoric items in columns 2-6. They differ from the anaphoric items in column 1 mainly in two respects. They provide cohesion for relatively small groups of sentences consisting of two to five adjacent sentences and the same grammatical items have different antecedents at various points in the paragraph.

It may also be remarked about items in 2-6 that either the antecedent of the anaphoric grammatical item or some other anaphoric item referring to that antecedent can be found in the preceding sentence. This fact is indicated by solid lines joining such items. In other words there is no anaphoric item in 2-6 whose antecedent cannot be found in a preceding adjacent sentence or traced through other anaphoric items in one or more preceding adjacent sentences. The only seeming exception is *this* in sentence (23) whose antecedent is removed by eight intervening sentences and the nearest anaphoric item carrying the same reference is removed by four sentences. The original antecedent of *this* of (23), however, is restated further on in the same sentence.[9] The device of repeating or restating the antecedent in the same sentence where the anaphoric item is found is used also in (10). The original antecedent is not present in sentence (9) although the latter contains the anaphoric *it* referring to the same antecedent as *this* of (10), Osmond's mind.

We could formulate a rule for the use of the anaphoric items of 2-6 in the paragraph analyzed. These items (items other than the ones marking the involvement of the participants) are used in the immediate neighborhood of either their antecedents or other anaphoric items referring to the same antecedents. A continuous line of anaphoric reference can be traced from one adjacent sentence to another in each case of an anaphoric item in 2-6. Where this is impossible, as in (23), the antecedent is restated in the sentence in which the anaphoric item appears. Conversely, when this continuous line of anaphoric reference stops it means that the next occurrence of the same anaphoric item will refer to a different antecedent.

The anaphoric items in column 1, on the other hand, do not seem to require a continuous line of anaphoric reference in order to refer to the same antecedent. These items appear to have the property of being able to function as cohesive ties across sentences which do not contain any mention of their referent. Incidentally, this different behavior of the third person personal pronouns depending on whether they mark the involvement of the participants in the narrative or not explains why some such pronouns

---

[9]   Cf. the discussion of *this* of (23) in section 3.2.

(together with the corresponding personal possessives) are indicated in column 1 and others in column 2.

Table 1 is to a large extent self-explanatory when used in conjunction with the description in section 4.2 since all relations marked by solid lines in the table were described in that section. Some of the relationships marked by dotted lines were also mentioned in section 4.2.

It should be pointed out that the patterns of anaphoric relations marked in Table 1 make it possible to distinguish many groupings of the sentences of the paragraph which are cohesive because of the presence in them of one kind of anaphoric item or another. In the table these groupings of sentences are shown separately but in the text of the paragraph they overlap and result in an intricate pattern of cohering sentences.

4.3.3. Grammatical cohesion: connectors

There are only three connectors which can be regarded as cohesive elements for the sentences in the paragraph. The connector *but* is used twice in that function — in both cases joining pairs of adjacent sentences, (1)/(2) and (34)/(35). *However* of (23) is the third sentence connector but it functions differently. It does not join two adjacent sentences. It joins (23) with the group of sentences (14)-(18). Sentence (23), where *however* is found, contains the anaphoric *this* whose antecedent is found in sentence (14) — that antecedent being anaphorically referred to in sentences (15)-(18). A restatement of the antecedent is also found in (23) following *this*. *However* is placed between the anaphoric *this* and the restated antecedent. These facts (Cf. Table 1, columns 2, 3, and 4a, sentences (14) through (23)) justify our considering *however* of (23) as a connector functioning as a cohesive tie across a number of sentences.[10]

---

[10] Gleason points out that this is quite a normal function for *however* which typically has a larger scope than *but*. With the occurrence of *however* there is a strong probability that it will function in a larger construction. *But* more often marks more immediate relations. *However* also has the property of being

4.3.4. Lexical cohesion

Six instances of lexical cohesion in adjacent sentences were discussed in section 4.2. The following are the pairs of adjacent sentences in the paragraph that display lexical cohesion: (1)/(2),
(14)/(15), (15)/(16), (23)/(24), (27)/(28), and (33)/(34).

There are also a few instances of lexical cohesive relation between
sentences which are separated by one or more intervening sentences. Table 2 illustrates the overall lexical cohesion in the paragraph studied. The solid and the dotted lines are used in the same
way as in Table 1. The lexical items are marked by an 'x' and the
anaphoric grammatical items referring to them by an '*'.

Either the noun *marriage* or a form of the verb *marry* are found in
sentences (1), (15), (19), and (21). The occurrence of the noun
marriage in (15) following the occurrence of the verb *had married*
in (1) can be seen as a cohesive relation between (1) and (15) since
the persons involved are the same in both cases. It is a weak cohesive tie as the two sentences are rather distant. The occurrences
of the verb forms *marry* and *married* in (19) and (21) respectively
provide lexical cohesion between (19) and (21) as well as between
these two and (15) together with (1).

Sentences (7) and (10) display lexical cohesion because they
contain two pairs of lexical cohesive items: *mind... mind* and
organ... instrument.[11] Sentences (19) and (21) display lexical
cohesion for the second time because of the word *ideas* found in
both sentences in parallel constructions. (19) and (21) cohere in
turn with (14) for the same reason. The group of lexically cohesive
sentences (14)-(19)-(21) can be extended by adding sentences (23)
and (24) since the latter two each contain the word *opinions* with
similar tendencies of collocation as the word *ideas*.

The lexical item *way* (in the sense of 'manner') is used in (25),

---

movable which *but* has not. The freedom of position of *however* makes possible
its close association with *this* and hence some indication of its scope (personal
communication, 1969).

[11] Cf. the discussion of the lexical items *mind, organ,* and *instrument* of (10)
in section 3.2.

TABLE 2

Overall lexical cohesion in James' paragraph

Sen. No.	MARRIAGE	OSMOND'S MIND	ISABEL'S IDEAS	WAY OF LOOKING AT LIFE	VARIOUS
1	married x				asked x
2					answer x
3					
4					
5					
6					
7		mind x / organ			
8		*			
9		*			
10		mind x / instr.			
11					
12					
13					
14			ideas x		said x
15	marriage x				told x / noticed x
16					noticed x
17					
18					
19	marry x		ideas x		
20					
21	married x		ideas x		
22					
23			opinions x		
24			opinions x		
25				way x	
26					
27				way x	
28				way x	
29				*	
30				*	
31					
32					
33					sense x
34					sense x
35					

(27), and (28) in collocations referring to partially identical concepts. Its three occurrences are therefore listed as cohesive.

In two instances lexical cohesion is extended through grammatical cohesion (Cf. sentences (7) through (10) and (25) through (30)).

4.4. SUMMARY DISCUSSION OF COHESION IN JAMES' PARAGRAPH

The selected passage from James' *The Portrait of a Lady* consists of 35 graphic sentences and 780 words. A passage of this length already allows us to perceive the varying use of the different kinds of cohesion and the patterning of cohesive choices over a portion of the text of the novel. At the same time the passage is still of a size that allows a detailed discussion and presentation of all cohesive elements studied.

Tables 3 and 4 represent a summary account of the grammatical versus lexical items found to function as cohesive ties for the adjacent sentences in the paragraph (Table 3) and between the clauses of the individual sentences (Table 4). Every occurrence of a grammatical cohesive item is marked by 'x' in the line corresponding to the number of the sentence or clause in which it appears. In most cases such an item functions as a cohesive tie between the sentence (clause) in which it is found and the preceding one. Some connectors, however, are found in the first of the two clauses they join. Only the second of a pair of lexical cohesive items is counted. In the table these lexical items are marked by 'X' and listed in the form in which they are found in the given sentence.

The most important observation that can be made about James' use of the two kinds of cohesion in the passage studied is that he depends heavily on grammatical cohesion. There are 115 items found to function cohesively for the pairs of sentences and of that number 107 items are grammatical and only 8 lexical. Similarly, there are 70 grammatical items supplying cohesion between the clauses and only 5 lexical ones.

With the exception of two connectors, in (2) and (35), all gram-

TABLE 3

Grammatical and lexical cohesion in adjacent sentences (James)

Sent. No.	GRAMMATICAL		LEXICAL
	anaphoric items	connectors	
1			
2	xx	x	X answer
3	x		
4	x		
5	x		
6	xxxx		
7	xx		
8	xxxxxx		
9	xxx		
10	xxx		XX mind, instrument
11	xx		
12	xxx		
13	xxxxx		
14	xxxx		
15	xxxxxxxx		X told
16	xxxxx		X noticed
17	xx		
18	xxxx		
19	xxxxxxxxx		
20	xxx		
21	x		
22	xxx		
23			
24	xx		X opinions
25	xxx		
26	xxxxxx		
27	xx		
28	x		X way
29	x		
30	xxx		
31	x		
32	x		
33	xx		
34	xxxx		X sense
35	xxxxxxx	x	
Total	105	2	
	107		8
items	115		

TABLE 4

Grammatical and lexical cohesion between clauses[12] (James)

Sent. and Cl. No.	GRAMMATICAL		LEXICAL
	anaphoric items	connectors	
(1)	(2)	(3)	(4)
1. 1			
2	x	x	
3	xx	x	
2. 1			
2		x	
3. 1			
2		x	
5. 1			
2	xx	x	
3	x	x	
6. 1			
2	xx		
3	xxx	x	
7. 1			
2	xx		X organ
8. 1			
2	xx		X lived
3	xx		X habitation
9. 1		x	
2	x		
3	x		
10. 1			
2	xx	x	X instrument
3	x		
11. 1			
2	x	x	
12. 1			
2		x	

---

[12] Since clauses cohere only within sentences, more clauses had to be taken into account to provide for the same number of pairs of cohering clauses as that of sentences in Table 3. The clauses are listed in Table 4 with the indication of the number of the sentence in which they are found (the first numeral) and of the order in which they follow in the sentence (the second numeral). Sentence (4) is a one-clause sentence and consequently has been omitted in the account.

is only one sentence, (23), which contains no anaphoric item which would supply a cohesive tie for that and the immediately preceding sentence. But sentence (23) displays no lexical cohesion with the preceding sentence either and it constitutes a break in the sequence where each sentence coheres directly with the preceding sentence.

When the overall cohesion in the paragraph is considered a few more lexical cohesive items can be listed since they can be viewed as supplying cohesion across a number of sentences. The sentences that cohere due to the presence in them of these items are relatively distant and they are few in number. Several of the lexical items listed in Table 2 derive their cohesive character at least in part from the fact that they are found with corresponding grammatical items the cohesiveness of which is often independent of the lexical items they accompany. For example, the several occurrences of the lexical items *ideas* and *opinions* are considered cohesive not only because they are repetitions or belong to a co-occurrence set but also, and more importantly, because they are grammatically related to either the pronoun *she* or the personal possessive *her* both of which have the same person as their anaphoric reference.

We could say therefore that James depends for the cohesion in the paragraph primarily and to a great extent on grammatical features — with anaphora playing the most important role. The lexical cohesion is relatively weak and to a considerable extent dependent on the strong grammatical cohesion.

The third person pronouns and personal possessives mark the large majority of the anaphoric relations in the paragraph. There are 82 third person pronouns and 11 personal possessives which are anaphoric, making the total of 93 cohesive items in this category. The large majority of these items (82 items) refer consistently throughout the paragraph to one of the two persons, Isabel and Osmond, whose relations are of primary concern in the chapter. They are considered here as the two participants in the narrative of the paragraph. The first of the two, Isabel, has the greater share in the 'actions' described in the passage and this is reflected in the representation of the anaphoric items in Table 1, column 1. At two points the lines representing the pronouns and personal possessives referring one to Isabel and one to Osmond are joined through the occurrences of *their* referring to both Isabel and Osmond.

The whole structure of the paragraph appears to be built around and to be dependent upon the almost continuous line of anaphoric reference realized by the occurrences of the third person pronouns and personal possessives that mark the involvement of the two participants (Cf. Table 1, column 1). The grammatical items listed in column 1 are found in all but two of the 35 sentences of the paragraph, from the first sentence to the last one. Every time an item of that group appears in the text of the passage it carries the same anaphoric reference. It might be said in other words that the anaphoric relations which signal the existence of a participant line on the semologic stratum provide a backbone for the cohesion of the whole paragraph.

The other grammatical and all lexical cohesive relations obtaining in the paragraph supplement and reinforce at various points the cohesion due to the almost continuous marking of participant involvement. They obtain in smaller groups of sentences only and

TABLE 5

Summary of cohesive items in adjacent sentences (James)

GRAMMATICAL				LEXICAL
107 (93%)				8 (7%)
Anaphora	pers. pronouns 82	93 (89%)	105 (98%)	
	pers. possess. 11			
	demonstratives 6	12 (11%)		
	determiners 4			
	substitutes 1			
	adverbs 1			
Connectors			2 (2%)	

the same exponents of the grammatical cohesive relations in this group (columns 2-6 in Table 1) have different reference in different parts of the text.

Table 5 presents a summary account of the various kinds of cohesive elements functioning for the adjacent sentences in James' paragraph. This table will be referred to in the next chapter, where the significance of the figures and percentages referring to the various cohesive items in the passage from James will be appreciated better when the table is compared with a similar table made for a passage from Hemingway.

The paragraph studied may be said to display a twofold cohesion. On the one hand the paragraph can be seen as a sequence of sentences each of which is joined with the sentence that it follows by one or more cohesive ties (Cf. section 3.2.). There is only one break in this sequence at sentence (23). On the other hand there can be discerned various patterns of cohesive relations which result in the cohesion of sentences that are not adjacent but are separated by one or more intervening sentences. Sentence (23), for example, coheres with sentence (21) due to lexical cohesion and with some earlier sentences because of the way the connector *however* relates that sentence with the group of sentences (14)-(18).

Some cohesive elements function simultaneously for pairs of adjacent sentences and groups of three or more sentences not all of which need to follow in an uninterrupted sequence. This brings up the problem of the cohesive range of grammatical and lexical items which will be discussed in detail in section 6.3.3. under the heading of the scope of cohesive elements. Examples from the Hemingway text will be used to illustrate.

We may conclude that the patterning of cohesive relations in James' paragraph is an intricate one and that all cohesive elements have to be considered before a full statement about the cohesion in the paragraph can be made. Although not all possible grammatical and lexical cohesive features are studied in this investigation, enough of them are included in the analysis to justify our considering the results of this examination as indicative of the nature of cohesion in the paragraph studied.

5

COHESION IN HEMINGWAY

5.1. INTRODUCTION

Several observations about the nature of cohesion in James' paras
graph have been made in the preceding chapter. It is difficult to
assess the full significance of these observations unless we can state
what alternative cohesive choices might have been made in a text
of a similar kind and length. M.A.K. Halliday notes that "a text
is meaningful not only in virtue of what it is but also in virtue
of what it might have been".[1] For the understanding of the
linguistic choices made in one literary text we should compare them
with the choices made in another literary text. As Halliday point-
out, "the most relevant exponent of the 'might have been' of a
work of literature is another work of literature."[2]

Hemingway's prose is considered to be stylistically considerably
different from James' and therefore promises to display different
cohesive features. For this reason a passage from the short story
"Big Two-Hearted River: Part I" by Ernest Hemingway was chosen. The text of the passage constitutes Appendix II. The passage
was taken from a short story because no novel by Hemingway
seems to contain a continuous narrative (with no dialogue inserted)
of a length that would match James' narrative paragraph of 35
sentences. Hemingway's passage consists of several paragraphs
but that is also one of the features which differentiate Hemingway's
prose from James'. The number of sentences was used as a criterion

[1] M. A. K. Halliday, "The Linguistic Study of Literary Texts", 302.
[2] Halliday, "The Linguistic Study of Literary Texts", 302-303.

in deciding the length of the passage because cohesive features are studied in this investigation primarily in relation to sentences.

Hemingway's passage contains 607 words which is less than the 780 words in James' paragraph. For this reason we will compare not the absolute numbers of various cohesive elements but their proportionate use in the two texts. This appears to be the correct procedure as the ratio of cohesive items to all words in the two texts is fairly close. There is one cohesive item per circa 7.5 words in Hemingway and one cohesive item per circa 6.8 words in James. This would indicate that the two passages do not differ greatly in the number of cohesive items used over a portion of the text, but that the difference lies in the different use of various kinds of cohesive features.

A detailed description of all cohesive features in Hemingway's passage will not be presented in this chapter. Such a description was given for James and therefore, it would be repetitious to do it for Hemingway too. In this chapter only the results of the examination of cohesion in Hemingway will be presented and some characteristic features of cohesion in the passage will be discussed and contrasted with those in James' paragraph.

5.2. COHESION IN ADJACENT SENTENCES

Table 6 presents a summary account of the grammatical versus lexical cohesive elements in adjacent sentences in Hemingway's passage. It is analogical to Table 3 in chapter 4 which presents a similar account for James. The difference in the use of the two kinds of cohesive items — which becomes apparent when we compare the two tables — is that Hemingway depends to a greater degree on lexical cohesion than James does. There are almost as many lexical as grammatical items functioning cohesively for the adjacent sentences in Hemingway. Some sentences contain three, and one sentence even four, lexical cohesive items. This is never the case in James. Also, in the Hemingway text the number of sentences containing three or more grammatical cohesive items

TABLE 6

Grammatical and lexical cohesion in adjacent setences (Hemingway)

Sent. No.	GRAMMATICAL		LEXICAL	
	anaphoric	connectors		
1				
2	xx		X	river
3	x			
4			XXX	water, bottom, current
5	xxxxx	x	XXX	hold steady, fast water, watched
6	x		XX	Nick, watched
7	xxxx		XXX	trout, watched, watched
8	x		XX	pool, trout
9	x			
10	xx	x	XX	see, big trout
11	x		XXX	Nick, looked, pool
12				
13				
14			X	stream
15	x			
16			X	trout
17	x		XX	tightened, trout
18	x			
19	x			
20	xx		XXXX	pebbly-bottomed, shallows, boulders, pool
21				
22	x			
23	xxxx			
24		x		
25	x		X	too heavy
26	x		XX	pack, weight
27	xxx		XXX	road, pack, heavy
28	x		X	road
29			X	walking up-hill
30				
31	xx		X	felt
32	xx			
33	x			
34			X	changed
35	x		X	burned
Total	41	3	38	
	44			
items	82			

is small in relation to the number of sentences containing one or two such items. In the James text the opposite is true.

There are some sentences in Table 6 for which no cohesive elements are indicated. This means that these sentences contain no grammatical nor lexical items causing them to cohere with the immediately preceding sentences. Their connectedness is established, however, with other preceding, although not adjacent, sentences through cohesive items which function across two or more sentence boundaries. This will be apparent when we examine the overall cohesion in section 5.4.

Sentences (12), (13), (21), and (30) constitute such breaks in the sequence of sentences which cohere each with the sentence immediately preceding. It may be noted that of the four only sentence (21) coincides with the beginning of a new paragraph. The sentences adjacent to the other five paragraph divisions in the studied passage display cohesion as pairs of adjacent sentences. It appears to be a feature of cohesion in Hemingway that usually there will be at least one cohesive tie for two sentences which are found on either side of a paragraph division. The breaks in cohesion in a sequence of adjacent sentences are more likely to occur inside a paragraph.[3]

In both texts the number of sentence connectors is small: two in James and three in Hemingway. The difference between the two texts might then be said to lie in the use of fewer grammatical

---

[3]   This does raise some questions about the nature of paragraph. According to Halliday the paragraph division coincides in some writers with the troughs and in some with the peaks of the strength of cohesion (lectures at the Linguistic Institute of the Linguistic Society of America, Summer, 1966). Hemingway seems to divide his sentences into paragraphs at the peaks of cohesive strength between sentences. Gleason notes that this convention of paragraphing is not peculiar to Hemingway and that paragraph is an arbitrary convention in English composition (personal communication, 1969). For example, it is seldom that a paragraph begins with a topic sentence and that all its other sentences develop the theme of the topic sentence. Some paragraphs do not contain a topic sentence at all. Writers often include in a paragraph sentences which otherwise would be unconnected and the reader generally assumes that what is inside a paragraph represents a connected whole. The attention of the reader and the writer (as well as the composition teacher) usually concentrates on the transitions between paragraphs, as the present study of Hemingway's passage indicates.

anaphoric items in Hemingway which is compensated for by the use of a greater number of lexical cohesive items. In other words, whereas James depends mainly on grammatical anaphora for the cohesion of adjacent sentences, Hemingway uses both kinds of cohesion in about the same proportion.

Table 7 should be compared with Table 5 of the preceding chapter. When this is done the difference between the cohesion in James and that in Hemingway is apparent. The cohesion between adjacent sentences in James is 93 percent grammatical and only 7 percent lexical. For Hemingway the corresponding figures are approximately 54 and 46 percent.

Both authors depend mainly on anaphora for grammatical cohesion and within anaphora on the third person pronouns and personal possessives. But Hemingway employs proportionately fewer pronouns and personal possessives and more determiners than James does. This fact appears to reflect the greater use of lexical cohesion in Hemingway. For example, the involvement of the participant in the narrative, Nick, is often realized by the lexical item *Nick*, reducing the number of instances when he is mentioned

TABLE 7

Summary of cohesive items in adjacent sentences (Hemingway)

GRAMMATICAL				LEXICAL
44 (54%)				38 (46%)
Anaphora	pers. pronouns 26	31 (76%)	41 (93%)	
	pers. possess. 5			
	demonstratives 0			
	determiners 9	10 (24%)		
	substitutes 0			
	adverbs 1			
Connectors			3 (7%)	

through the pronominal anaphoric items. The number of anaphoric determiners is also related in some degree to the number of lexical cohesive items.

Another difference in the cohesion of the two passages is in the use of the demonstrative pronouns. There are six such items in James' paragraph and none in the passage from Hemingway. It will be remembered that the demonstratives *this* and *that* were used in James to refer to antecedents which could not always be stated exactly and that they were used in conjunction with other anaphoric items referring to the same antecedents. This resulted in a complex patterning of grammatical anaphoric relations (Cf. Table 1, columns 2-4). The absence of these not so definite anaphoric items in Hemingway's passage results in a simpler and clearer pattern of grammatical cohesive relations.

5.3. COHESION BETWEEN CLAUSES

Table 8 contains an account of grammatical and lexical items found to function cohesively for the clauses of Hemingway's passage. Table 8 is constructed analogously to Table 4 in the chapter on cohesion in James. The two tables should be compared.

When cohesion between clauses is examined certain parallels in the distribution of cohesive elements in both Hemingway and James can be observed. There is proportionately less lexical cohesion between clauses than between sentences in each text. But in Hemingway lexical items still constitute about one fourth of all cohesive elements, whereas in James they make only one sixteenth of all cohesive items. These two observations reinforce each other. First, there is proportionately more lexical cohesion in Hemingway than there is in James whether the units that cohere are adjacent sentences or whether they are clauses. Second, in each text as we move from sentences to clauses the use of lexical cohesion is proportionately smaller.

Another parallel in the two texts is that connectors play a greater part in the cohesion of clauses than in that of sentences. In both

TABLE 8

Grammatical and lexical cohesion between clauses (Hemingway)

Sent. and Cl. No.	GRAMMATICAL		LEXICAL
	anaphoric items	connectors	
(1)	(2)	(3)	(4)
1. 1			
2	x	x	
3	x	xx	
4. 1			
2		x	X current
5. 1		x	
2	xx		
7. 1			
2	x	x	XX watched, pool
14. 1			
2		x	
3	x	x	
16. 1		x	
2			
3	xx	x	X shadow
4	x	x	
5	x		
6	xx	xx	XX shadow, stream
7	x	x	XX stream, surface
8	x	x	X current
17. 1			
2		x	
19. 1			
2	x	x	
20. 1			
2	x	x	
21. 1			
2	x	x	X railway track
23. 1			
2	xx		X pack
3	xx		X shoulder straps
4	xxx	x	XX shoulders, tumpline
26. 1			
2	xx	x	
3	x		
4	xx	x	X fire-scarred
30. 1			

(1)	(2)	(3)	(4)	
2		x		
3		x	X	Nick
33. 1				
2	x	x	X	baggage man
3		x		
34. 1				
2			X	burned over
3	x	x		
37. 1				
2	x			
42. 1				
2	x			
46. 1				
2	x	x	X	water
47. 1				
2	x			
Total	35	28		
	63		19	
items	82			

texts connectors are used mainly to indicate clause cohesion.

One more parallel in the nature of cohesion in the two texts can be seen in the fact that pronouns account proportionately for more cohesive relations between James' clauses than between Hemingway's. This parallels what was observed when sentences were considered. In James' clauses pronouns still constitute the largest group of grammatical cohesive items (there are 35 pronouns and 21 connectors) but in Hemingway's clauses anaphoric elements in the category of pronouns, 20 in number, give way to connectors whose count is 28. The part played by actual pronouns in Hemingway's clauses will be even smaller when we consider that out of the 20 instances of cohesive ties due to anaphora in the group of personal pronouns 10 are realized as zero anaphora. There are no instances of zero anaphora in James' clauses.

The above parallels in the different use of the various cohesive items in both texts as we move from sentence to clause cohesion have a double significance. They reinforce our earlier statements (in section 5.2.) about the differences in the nature of cohesion in Hemingway and in James, and at the same time they suggest that the shift in emphasis on particular kinds of cohesive items may be common to more than one kind of texts. The greater use of connectors and the smaller use of lexical cohesive items, for example, appear to characterize clause cohesion as contrasted with cohesion between sentences.

5.4.   OVERALL COHESION IN THE PASSAGE

It was noted in the preceding chapter that the line of anaphoric reference that marked participant involvement provided a backbone for the cohesion in James' paragraph. That line depended wholly on grammatical anaphora as it consisted only of the third person pronouns and personal possessives. It ran through the whole length of the paragraph.

There are some similarities and differences in this respect in Hemingway's passage. A line of anaphoric reference marking participant involvement can be also discerned. As in James it runs through the length of the passage and continues beyond it in both directions (cf. Table 9).

Unlike the situation in James, however, the line is due to the occurrences of both grammatical and lexical items which alternate fairly evenly throughout the passage. There is only one group of three consecutive sentences in which the participant is mentioned by pronouns only. In other cases a sentence or two adjacent sentences in which the participant is referred to by means of the third person masculine pronoun, are preceded or followed by sentences in which the participant is mentioned by name, the lexical item *Nick*.

Besides being realized by both lexical and grammatical items the anaphoric line marking participant involvement in Hemingway's passage differs also from such a line in James in that it has gaps in several places. These gaps are due to sentences which do not contain any mention of the participant. It will be remembered that in James the line of participant involvement could be traced in all

TABLE 9

Overall cohesion in Hemingway: some grammatical and lexical items

Sen. No.	NICK	RIVER	TROUT	BRIDGE	LOOK-SEE	PACK	WALK	ROAD
1	Nick	river		bridge	looked		|walked	
2	|	river		|	|		|—|	
3	|	(it)		bridge	|		|	
4	Nick	water	trout	|	looked		|	
5	(he)	water	(they)	|	watched		|	
6	Nick	|	(them)	|	watched		|	
7	(he)	pool	trout	bridge	watched		|	
8	|	pool	trout	|	|		|	
9	Nick	|	(them)	|	see		|	
10	(he)	pool	trout	|	saw		|	
11	Nick	pool	|	bridge	looked		|	
12	|	|	|	|	|		|	
13	|	stream	|	|	|		|	
14	Nick	stream	trout	|	looked		|	
15	|	|	(they)	|	|		|	
16	|	stream	trout	bridge	|		|	
17	Nick's	|	trout		|		|	
18	(he)	|			|		|	
19	(he)	stream			looked		|	
20	|	(it)					|	
21	Nick					pack	walked	
22	(he)					|	|	
23	(he)					pack	|	
24	|					(it)	|	
25	|					(it)	|	
26	(he)					pack	walked	road
27	(he)					pack	walked	road
28	|					|	|	|
29	|					|	walking	|
30	Nick					|	|	|
31	(he)					|	|	|
32	(him)					|	|	|
33	(he)					pack	|	|
34	|						|	|
35	|						|	|
36	(he)						|	|
37	(he)						hiked	road
38	|						|	road
39	Nick						went on	|
40	|							road

sentences except one. In Hemingway, however, most of these gaps are bridged by the lexical cohesion due to the several sets of cohering lexical items found in tight groups of sentences.

Table 9 represents the distribution of the more important lexical and grammatical items in forty consecutive sentences of Hemingway's passage. Because of limited space not all cohesive items are indicated. For any given sentence only one item is listed (grammatical items are enclosed in parentheses). In some instances there are two or more grammatical items or items from the same lexical set found in one sentence. The capitalized words at the head of each column are meant as cover terms for the several items belonging to individual lexical sets. Grammatical items are indicated when they function cohesively in conjunction with lexical items and only in the absence of the latter. The vertical dotted lines join items whose presence makes non-adjacent sentences cohere. The horizontal dotted lines mark the groups of sentences with a concentration of cohesive relations due to the presence in these sentences of several items of the same lexical set or sets.

A general observation about Table 9 is that large groups of sentences cohere due to the occurrences of items from several lexical sets (often the repetition of the same item) and that grammatical cohesion functions mainly as a reinforcing and supplementing factor. This is an important characteristic of cohesion in Hemingway. It is different from James where grammatical cohesion was found to provide the basis for the cohesiveness of the whole passage.

It is apparent from Table 9 that the largest group of sentences (including most sentences in the passage) coheres because of the anaphoric line marking participant involvement. Within that large group there can be discerned two or three groups of sentences displaying stronger cohesive ties because of the presence in them of items from several lexical sets. It should be noted that items creating lexical cohesion in one group are generally absent from another group of sentences which coheres due to another set or other sets of items.

Sentences (1) through (19) display strong lexical cohesion because of the frequent occurrences of items from the lexical sets RIVER, TROUT, BRIDGE, and LOOK-SEE. The first three sets might also be seen as one lexical set. The items from these three sets realize what might be considered as partly participant (*trout*) and partly circumstance or location (*river, stream, pool, bridge*) categories of the semologic stratum. The lexical set LOOK-SEE is closely related with the other three sets and with the corresponding portion of the anaphoric line marking participant involvement since it represents the actions of the participant *Nick*. This set of synonymous verbs realizes the event line of the semologic stratum consisting of several occurrences of the same action. Or perhaps it would be more accurate to say that the same single action on the semologic stratum is realized morphologically through several occurrences of the synonymous verbs *look, watch,* and *see.*

Two or three more groups of closely related sentences due to lexical cohesion can be turned up in the passage. They are sentences (21)-(33), (21)-(39), and (26)-(40). These groups partly overlap and can also be considered as one group of cohesive sentences similar to the group (1)-(19).

It might be mentioned that such groups of sentences cohering due to items from a lexical set or sets can be found in the remainder of the short story. Some of these groups are those whose lexical cohesion is built each around one of the following items: *the pine plain, cigarette* and *smoke, grasshopper, walk* (*walking*), *pine trees* (*branches*), *meadow, camp, tent, hungry, remember, coffee, sleep,* in this order.

5.5. HEMINGWAY'S CHARACTERISTIC LEXICAL COHESION

It was noted in section 5.4. that much of the lexical cohesion in Hemingway is due to the repetition of the same lexical item. But what is even more characteristic of this type of cohesion is that a lexical item is introduced in one sentence and then it is repeated in the immediately following sentence so that the two occurrences of such item (each occurrence in one sentence) form a pair of cohesive lexical elements and provide a link between the two sentences.

In the passage studied such pairs are *river-river, water-water, pool-pool, stream-stream, trout-trout, watched-watched, see-saw, pack-pack, walked-walked,* and *road-road* (Cf. Table 9).

A perfect example of this kind of cohesion can be found in a passage of three paragraphs from Hemingway's novel *For Whom the Bell Tolls* which is quoted below with the relevant items italicized and the sentences numbered so that they can be referred to in Table 10 which follows the passage.

(1) Now *in the night* he lay and waited for the girl to come to
(2) him. There was no wind now and *the pines* were still *in the*
(3) *night.* The trunks of *the pines* projected from the snow that covered all the ground, and he *lay* in the robe feeling the suppleness of the bed under him that he had made, his legs stretched long against the warmth of the robe, the air sharp and cold on *his head* and in his nostrils as he breathed.
(4) Under *his head,* as he *lay* on his side, was the bulge of the trousers and the coat that he had wrapped around his shoes to make a pillow and against his side was the cold metal of the big automatic *pistol* he had taken from the holster when he undressed and fastened by its halyard to his right
(5) wrist. He pushed *the pistol* away and settled deeper into the robe as he watched, across *the snow,* the dark break in the
(6) rocks that was the entrance to *the cave.* The sky was clear and there was enough light reflected from *the snow* to see the trunks of the trees and the bulk of the rocks where *the cave* was.
(7)   Earlier in the evening he had taken the ax and gone outside of the cave and walked through *the* new *snow* to the edge of the clearing and cut down a small spruce *tree.*
(8) In the dark he had dragged *it,* butt first, to the lee of the
(9) *rock* wall. There close to *the rock,* he had held *the tree* upright, holding the trunk firm with one hand, and, holding the ax-haft close to the head had lopped off all the *boughs*

(10) until he had a *pile of them*. Then, leaving *the pile of boughs*, he had laid the bare pole of the trunk down in the snow and gone into the cave to get *a slab of wood* he had seen against

(11) the wall. With *this slab* he scraped the ground clear of the snow along the rock wall and then picked up his *boughs* and shaking them clean of snow laid them in rows, like

(12) overlapping plumes, until he had a *bed*. He put the pole across the foot of the *bough bed* to hold the branches in place and pegged it firm with two pointed pieces of wood he split from the edge of *the slab*.

(13)   Then he carried *the slab* and the ax back into the cave, ducking under the blanket as he came in, and leaned them both against the wall.[4]

The above passage displays lexical cohesion of the strongest kind. Not only are the same items repeated in close proximity (in adjacent sentences) but they often are found in the same or parallel constructions which emphasizes their identical reference. Some examples of the pairs of identical or parallel constructions containing the lexical items in question are, *in the night-in the night, on his head-under his head, he lay-as he lay, across the snow-from the snow, the boughs… a pile of them-the pile of boughs*. Several pairs of adjacent sentences contain two cohesive links of this type making this cohesion even stronger. Table 10 represents this characteristic kind of Hemingway's use of lexical cohesion in the passage quoted above.

---

[4] Ernest Hemingway, *For Whom the Bell Tolls* (New York, 1940), 258-259.

TABLE 10
Characteristic use of lexical cohesion in Hemingway

Sen. No.	Pairs of cohesive items
1	(in the) night
	↕
2	(in the) night
	(the) pines
	↕
3	(trunks of the) pines
	(on his) head (he) lay
	↕ ↕
4	(under his) head (as he) lay
	(the big...) pistol
	↕
5	(the) pistol
	(across the) snow (the) cave
	↕ ↕
6	(from the) snow (the) cave
	↕ ↕
7	(the new) snow (the) cave
	(a small spruce) tree
	↕
8	(it)
	↑ (the) rock (wall)
	↓ ↕
9	(the) tree (the) rock
	(the) boughs... (a) pile of (them)
	└──────↕──────┘
10	(the) pile of boughs
	(a) slab (of wood)
	↕
11	(this) slab
	(his) boughs... (a) bed
	└────↕────┘
12	(the) bough bed
	(the) slab
	↕
13	(the) slab

6

IMPLICATIONS AND CONCLUSIONS

6.1. COHESIVE FEATURES IN LITERARY TEXTS

In Chapters 3 through 5 a technique was developed and applied to the study of cohesion in literary prose texts. The examination of cohesive features in the passages from James and Hemingway shows that literary texts do display cohesion as it is conceived of in this investigation. The grammatical and lexical features listed under the heading of cohesion in section 3.2. were found to be present and to function cohesively in the texts analyzed.

The evidence of the examination is strongly suggestive that in a sequence of sentences forming a literary prose text there will be a certain density of cohesive items. There is one cohesive item per circa 6.8 words in James and one per circa 7.5 words in Hemingway. The two texts have not been found to differ greatly in the number of cohesive items used over a portion of the text. They differ considerably, however, in the proportion of the lexical and of the grammatical items used to provide cohesion. This may indicate that there is an interdependence between the number of the two kinds of cohesive items employed in a text. The writer's freedom may lie not so much in how large the total number of cohesive elements he has to use in a text will be as in the choice among the various kinds of cohesion that he can employ. He may, for example, rely more heavily either on lexical or on grammatical cohesion. The patterning of cohesive choices within each of the two kinds of cohesion seems also to be more open to the writer's option.

When cohesion between sentences is compared with that between clauses in a given text, clauses show greater dependence on grammatical items for their cohesion than do sentences. The dependence on lexical cohesion is proportionately smaller in clauses (cf. section 5.3.). At the same time as we move from sentences to clauses the use of connectors increases. The role played by connectors in the texts analyzed is very small when sentences are considered but connectors are found to provide cohesive ties between a large number of clauses (cf. Tables 4 and 8).

While anaphora accounts for much of the grammatical cohesion in the texts examined, this is due almost exclusively to the occurrences of only three exponents of anaphora: pronouns, determiners, and personal possessives. Substitutes, adverbs, and submodifiers are either absent from these texts or limited to the occurrence of one item in a given passage (cf. Tables 5 and 7).

6.2. COHESIVE CHOICES AND STYLE

The two passages examined in this study were deliberately chosen from James and Hemingway because the writings of the two authors are considered stylistically different. It was noted in Chapter 1 that many stylistic problems can be related to the realizational relationships between the semologic and the grammatic (i.e. morphologic) strata. Since cohesive relations are marked by those grammatical and lexical features that realize semologic structure on the morphologic stratum a difference in style should also be reflected in a difference in cohesive choices. We began with the assumption that if we construct an adequate descriptive framework for the study of cohesion in literary texts, its application to the examination of two stylistically different texts should yield results that will reflect different cohesive choices in these texts. This assumption has been confirmed by the results of the examination of cohesion in the selected passages from James and Hemingway.

The authors studied have been shown to differ markedly in the use of the two kinds of cohesion, grammatical and lexical. James' heavy dependence on grammatical cohesion is paralleled by his infrequent use of lexical cohesion (cf. section 4.4.). There are, for example, only 8 lexical items found to function cohesively in the pairs of adjacent sentences as compared with 107 grammatical cohesive items. Hemingway's use of the two kinds of cohesion is characterized by his greater dependence on lexical cohesion. There are almost as many lexical as grammatical items functioning cohesively for the adjacent sentences in the passage from Hemingway. This quantitative difference in the use of the grammatical versus lexical cohesion reflects the different choices made by each author in regard to the realization of semologic structure. In English there is considerable freedom in the manner in which semologic units can be realized morphologically. Assuming that the same or similar options were open to both writers the marked difference in the cohesive choices can be seen as reflecting the considerable difference in the writers' style.

The overall quantitative difference in the use of both kinds of cohesion is not the only distinguishing feature of the passages examined. The passages differ also in the patterning of cohesive choices. In the passage from James, for example, almost all grammatical cohesion is due to anaphora, and more specifically to the occurrences of personal pronouns and personal possessives most of which signal the involvement of the participants. The participant involvement is marked almost continuously throughout the passage and the line marking this participant involvement constitutes the backbone for the cohesion of the whole passage. In other words James' 35 sentences display connectedness mainly because of the occurrences of the third person pronouns and personal possessives. There are no other cohesive items in the text which by themselves provide connectedness for any larger groups of sentences. The burden of supplying cohesion is carried to a very large extent by just one kind of cohesive items: the anaphoric pronouns and possessives.

The semologic actions and circumstances can be seen as connected in James' passage mostly through their connection with the participant line. They are dependent for their connectivity on the existing connectedness of the participant line. This may be a reflection of

James' preoccupation with the person of the heroine, Isabel, expressing itself in the subordination of everything else to that person.

Although the anaphoric line marking participant involvement can also be traced through the whole length of the Hemingway text, this line is different in some respects from that in the James text. It is not a continuous line running through nearly all the sentences of the text and it is not realized by pronominal elements only. The lexical item *Nick* alternates with the pronouns *he* and *him*. The line is broken at many points by sentences containing no mention of the participant, and the largest groups of adjacent sentences which cohere because of the mention of the participant include four sentences only. At the same time, slightly larger groups of sentences (including up to seven sentences at a time) cohere because of the lexical cohesion dependent on occurrences of items in the sets — RIVER, TROUT, and PACK — all of which realize circumstantial sememes. This may reflect Hemingway's almost equal emphasis on the person of the participant and on the circumstances in which his experience takes place.

A look at Table 9 of Chapter 5 demonstrates that there are groups of lexical items, supplemented by a few grammatical ones, each of which realize one group of events and circumstances. These items provide cohesion to two groups of sentences into which the text seems divided. The cohesion these groups supply parallels that supplied by the anaphoric line of participant involvement. Sentences (1)-(20) display cohesion due to one set of items (listed under the headings of RIVER, TROUT, BRIDGE, LOOK-SEE) and sentences (21)-(40) display cohesion due to a different set of items (PACK, ROAD, WALK). WALK is also realized in the first group but only once at the beginning of that group and can be seen as a cohesive link between the two groups of sentences.

In James no such groups of cohesive items indicated the existence of a clear line of circumstances or events which would show connectedness in addition to that dependent on the participant line.

The examination of the passages by Hemingway established a characteristic manner in which the writer uses lexical cohesion.

Hemingway's characteristic lexical cohesion has been shown to depend on the introduction of a lexical item (sometimes more than one) in one sentence or clause and then the repetition of the same item (items) or the use of items from the same lexical set in the immediately following sentence or clause. These cohering lexical items are usually found in close proximity. The following sentences from Hemingway's text will illustrate (the relevant items are italicized):

(1) Nick looked at the burned-over stretch of hillside, where he had expected to find the scattered houses of the town and then walked down the railroad track to the bridge over the *river*.

(2) The *river* was there.

(4) Nick looked down into the clear, brown water, colored from the pebbly bottom, and *watched* the trout keeping themselves steady in the current with wavering fins.

(5) As he *watched* them they changed their positions by quick angles, only to hold steady in the fast water again.

(6) Nick *watched* them a long time.

(7) He *watched* them holding themselves with their noses into the current, many trout in deep, fast moving water...[1]

In the sequence (4)-(7) only the lexical item *watch* has been italicized for ease of reference. There are, however, other lexical items cohering across sentence or clause boundaries: *current — fast — water — current — fast moving water*; *keeping steady — hold steady — holding*.

The examination of James' text, on the other hand, has shown

[1] Ernest Hemingway, "Big Two-Hearted River: Part I", *The Short Stories of Ernest Hemingway* (New York: Charles Scribner's Sons, 1953), 209.

a limited use of lexical cohesion, but instead a very complex pattern of cohesive relations depending on grammatical cohesive items (cf. Table 1 and the accompanying discussion in section 4.3.). It has also been shown that James carefully observes the rules of anaphoric reference. Due to this fact it is usually possible to establish unambiguously the antecedents of the various grammatical anaphoric items despite their high frequency in the text and the little assistance the reader can derive from the scarce items of lexical cohesion. Occasionally, however, as with the demonstrative pronouns *this* and *that*, it is not always clear what the exact referents of certain anaphoric items are.

James' carefully constructed but quite involved and complex grammatical cohesion dependent almost entirely on anaphora makes the semantic interpretation of his text more involved and difficult than that of the passage by Hemingway. A more balanced combination of lexical and grammatical cohesion, together with the considerable redundancy resulting from the use of lexical cohesion in the manner discussed above, supplies the text by Hemingway with simple and clear cohesion.

6.3. COHESIVE FEATURES AND DISCOURSE STRUCTURE

It was suggested in section 2.3.2. that there exists a close relationship between the patterning of cohesive features in a text and the semologic structure (representing discourse structure) of the text. We will discuss below some of the implications that the present study of cohesion may have for the investigation of English discourse structure.

6.3.1. Participant line

In both of the passages studied the largest group of cohesive items forms a line of anaphoric reference that goes through the whole length of the passage, a sort of backbone for the text. This line of cohesive items points to the existence on the semologic stratum of the participant line.

In the text by James, except for the initial occurrence of the proper name introducing the principal participant, this line consists wholly of third person pronouns and personal possessives. In the text by Hemingway, both proper nouns and personal pronouns are used interchangeably and within sentences there are cases of zero anaphora also used to signal participant involvement. One can therefore postulate on the basis of this particular patterning of cohesive choices the existence of a participant line which is clearly marked in English narrative texts.

This participant involvement may be signalled by nominal and pronominal items as well as by zero anaphora. The latter, however, at least in the texts studied, is restricted to clauses within sentences. It was never found to occur across sentence boundaries.

A fourth way that participant involvement is signalled in the texts studied is by inalienable possession. It should be noted in this connection that grammatical constructions alone do not always indicate what are the relevant semologic units and that the patterning of cohesive features may often give a better indication about the nature of those units. In the stratificational framework the sememe PARTICIPANT may be realized in an oblique way, that is, the head of the grammatical construction does not always correspond to the relevant semologic unit.

It was noted in connection with sentence (1) from James' passage, *Isabel's cheek burned when she asked herself if she had really married on a factitious theory, in order to do something finely appreciable with her money.*, that the grammatical unit *Isabel's cheek* realizes the semologic unit ISABEL rather than CHEEK. This is so although *cheek* is grammatically the head of the construction. This is borne out by the fact that the second involvement of the participant is realized in the following clause by the anaphoric *she* rather than *it*.

Another such example is found in James' sentence (7), *She had not been mistaken about the beauty of his mind; she knew that organ perfectly now.* Here the study of cohesive items leads to a correct establishment of the pertinent semologic units. Both grammatical and lexical cohesion point out that in the phrase *the beauty of his mind* the lexical item *mind* realizes the relevant semologic unit although *beauty* is the head of the grammatical construction. *Organ*, an item from the same lexical set, reinforced by anaphoric *that* coheres with *mind* and not with *beauty*.

A similar example is found in Hemingway's text, sentences (17) and (18): *Nick's heart tightened as the trout moved. He felt all the old feeling.* Again it is *Nick* rather than *heart* which points to the relevant semologic unit. *He*, not *it*, is the appropriate anaphoric item.

To return to sentence (1) of James' text, we note that the example *Isabel's cheek burned* can also be viewed as a paraphrase of:

> *Isabel blushed*

or *Isabel turned red*

This points up the fact that one entity on the semologic stratum may be realized by a variety of constructions on the grammatic stratum. The study of cohesive features thus indicates the existence of units of the semologic stratum which are not always discoverable otherwise.

It can be noted here that Fillmore[2] distinguishes between the deep-structure subject and the surface-structure subject, relating this distinction to the traditional one between 'logical' and 'grammatical' subject.[3] He also points out that conversion to genitive is a matter of surface structure.[4] Furthermore he applies his notion of "promotion", by which he means that a subordinate element in a grammatical construction may get "promoted" and become the head of that construction. This he illustrates for cases of inalienable possession where the thing possessed belongs to a small closed set such as body parts and kin.[5] Some of Fillmore's examples are quite similar to those discovered in the texts under examination. It should be noted that the examples from James and Hemingway,

---

[2] Charles Fillmore, "The Case for Case", *Universals of Linguistic Theory*, ed. by Emmon Bach and Robert T. Harms (New York, 1968), 1-88.
[3] Fillmore, "The Case for Case", 16.
[4] Fillmore, "The Case for Case", 50.
[5] Fillmore, "The Case for Case", 61-81.

Isabel's cheek, Nick's heart, and *his mind,* represent cases of inalienable possession.

It was noted in section 6.2. that the anaphoric line signalling participant involvement in Hemingway's passage is a broken one. The sentences which contain no cohesive items signalling the involvement of the participant mark the breaks in that line (cf. Table 9, column NICK). Table 11 shows the ordering of both kinds of sentences.

TABLE 11

Sentences with and without the participant involvement marked (Hemingway)

A	B	A	B	A	B
(1)		(14)		(27)	
—	(2)	—	(15)	—	(28)
—	(3)	—	(16)	—	(29)
(4)		(17)		(30)	
(5)		(18)		(31)	
(6)		(19)		(32)	
(7)		—	(20)	(33)	
—	(8)	(21)		—	(34)
(9)		(22)		—	(35)
(10)		(23)		(36)	
(11)		—	(24)	(37)	
—	(12)	—	(25)	—	(38)
—	(13)	(26)		(39)	
				—	(40)

The first column (A) in Table 11 contains sentences which cohere because of the presence in them of cohesive items signalling the involvement of the participant. The second column (B) contains sentences where the participant involvement is not signalled.

Upon examination it appears that the sentences of column B are circumstantial and descriptive and are tied into the narrative more loosely than are the sentences of column A. They can be removed from the text completely without essentially affecting the progress of the narrative. Of course, when removing these sentences sometimes adjustment in anaphora and paragraph division would have to be made. For example, here are sentences (1) to (6), forming the first paragraph in Hemingway's text:

(1) Nick looked at the burned-over stretch of hillside, where he had expected to find the scattered houses of the town and then walked down the railroad track to the bridge over the river.
(2) The river was there.
(3) It swirled against the log spiles of the bridge.
(4) Nick looked down into the clear, brown water, colored from the pebbly bottom, and watched the trout keeping themselves steady in the current with wavering fins.
(5) As he watched them they changed their positions by quick angles, only to hold steady in the fast water again.
(6) Nick watched them a long time.

We note that sentences (2) and (3) can be removed without changing the course of the narrative. The new text would then read:

(1) Nick looked at the burned-over stretch of hillside, where he had expected to find the scattered houses of the town and then walked down the railroad track to the bridge over the river.
(4) Nick looked down into the clear, brown water, colored from the pebbly bottom, and watched the trout keeping themselves steady in the current with wavering fins.
(5) As he watched them they changed their positions by quick angles, only to hold steady in the fast water again.
(6) Nick watched them a long time.

Most of the sentences in column B — although not marked for participant involvement — cohere in other ways with adjacent sentences. But four of them, sentences (12), (13), (20), and (29), show zero cohesion[6] with either the preceding or the following

---

[6] That is, 'zero cohesion' in regard to the cohesive features studied in this book. One could say that these sentences cohere with those for which we have estab-

sentences. Here again the study of cohesion points up sentences which are less closely involved in the narrative and which can either be removed from the narrative completely or be moved to certain other positions in the narrative without affecting its course. An examination of part of the paragraph containing sentences (28) and (29) will illustrate. Below is the relevant section as it appears in the text:

(26) He had his leather rod-case in his hand and leaning forward to keep the weight of the pack high on his shoulders he walk-ed along the road that paralleled the railway track, leaving the burned town behind in the heat, and then turned off around a hill with a high, fire-scarred hill on either side onto a road that went back into the country.

(27) He walked along the road feeling the ache from the pull of the heavy pack.

(28) The road climbed steadily.

(29) It was hard work walking up-hill.

(30) His muscles ached and the day was hot, but Nick felt happy.

(31) He felt he had left everything behind, the need for thinking, the need to write, other needs.

(32) It was all back of him.

Besides the possibility of removing sentences (28) and (29) com-pletely from the narrative without affecting its flow, these sentences may also be reordered in relation to other sentences of the section. For example, sentence (29) can be moved to a position preceding (28), or both (28) and (29) can together be inserted between sen-tences (26) and (27). With the latter rearrangement the relevant section would now read:

(26) He had his leather rod-case in his hand and leaning forward to keep the weight of the pack high on his shoulders he walked

---

lished zero cohesion through sequence of tenses, for example, but this alone seems to be a weak cohesive link.

along the road that paralleled the railway track, leaving the burned town behind in the heat, and then turned off around a hill with a high, fire-scarred hill on either side onto a road that went back into the country.

(28) The road climbed steadily.

(29) It was hard work walking up-hill.

(27) He walked along the road feeling the ache from the pull of the heavy pack.

(30) His muscles ached and the day was hot, but Nick felt happy.

(31) He felt he had left everything behind, the need for thinking, the need to write, other needs.

(32) It was all back of him.

In fact, after making the latter rearrangement, we feel that we have improved upon Hemingway. That is, we have suggested a new arrangement which is actually more characteristic of Hemingway's manner of establishing cohesion. Each sentence now contains a lexical item which coheres, in the sentence immediately following, with the same lexical item or with one from the same set, e.g. (a) road — (the) road, walking — walked, (the) ache — ached, felt — felt.

Again the study of cohesion reveals a feature of English discourse structure, namely that some sentences in a discourse are less strictly ordered than others and that such sentences may be reordered without affecting the narrative flow of the text. This observation is given even more substance when we consider the findings of Labov and Waletzky in connection with their study of simple, spoken English narratives.[7]

Labov and Waletzky studied spoken narrative of a casual and unplanned sort using the clause as the unit of discourse. They found

---

[7] William Labov and Joshua Waletzky, "Narrative Analysis: Oral Versions of Personal Experience", *Essays on the Verbal and Visual Arts*, ed. by June Helm (Seattle, 1967), 12-44. Labov incorporated most of the article in a later chapter on "The Transformation of Experience in Narrative Syntax" which is Chapter 9 of William Labov, *Language in the Inner City* (Philadelphia: University of Pennsylvania Press, 1972).

that the clauses of the various narratives could be classified as (1) narrative clauses, that is, those that are locked in position or strictly related in temporal order with other adjacent clauses, (2) free clauses capable of ranging over the whole narrative, and (3) restricted clauses whose range is limited to some positions only. The discovery that clauses of a spoken text may be divided into those that can be reordered and those that cannot is supported by our findings. Here sentences rather than clauses were the units examined since it was written text that we were concerned with. We should expect written texts, and especially literary texts, to be much more carefully structured than are spoken narratives of the kind which Labov and Waletzky examined. Yet in our text we discover that some sentences can be reordered. These sentences will include the ones that are not joined through realizations of the main participant line as well as some of those which display no cohesion with the adjacent sentences.

6.3.2. Event line

Gleason has pointed out that the organization of the event line and the identification of the participants are two of the systems of structure that hold discourse together.[8] While the patterning of cohesive features in the texts by both James and Hemingway clearly reveal the existence of the participant line, the cohesive features studied do not so clearly indicate the event line. It should be remembered, however, that sequence of tenses, a cohesive feature that might have more relation to the event line, was not included in this study.

Nonetheless, for the Hemingway text one thing may be stated. An examination of Table 9 shows for the column LOOK-SEE and for the column WALK a line of repeated items or of items belonging to the same lexical set. Since these items realize semologic actions the fact of their forming a set of cohering verbs establishes connection of the semologic actions realized by them. It ought to

[8] H. A. Gleason, Jr., "Contrastive Analysis in Discourse Structure", 58.

be remembered that an event line consists of actions with connections between them. While connections may be signalled by connectors such as temporals, the present study of cohesion shows that in English, connections between semologic actions may also be signalled by lexical cohesion of the verbs that realize these actions on the morphologic stratum. For example, the sequence of sentences containing cohering verbs in Table 9, *looked — looked — watched — see — saw — looked — looked,* realizes part of the event line of the narrative.

6.3.3. Scope of cohesive elements

It should be noted that the cohesive range of an item, grammatical or lexical, may vary from two adjacent sentences through three or more adjacent sentences to several non-adjacent sentences or groups of sentences. The following selection from Hemingway will illustrate this. The selected lexical cohesive items, *bottom, pool, trout, see, looked, stream,* have been italicized. The occurrences of each item should be considered separately.

(8) At the *bottom* of the *pool* were the big *trout.*

(9) Nick did not *see* them at first.

(10) Then he *saw* them at the *bottom* of the *pool,* big *trout* looking to hold themselves on the gravel *bottom* in a varying mist of gravel and sand, raised in spurts by the current.

(11) Nick *looked* down into the *pool* from the bridge.

(12) It was a hot day.

(13) A kingfisher flew up the *stream.*

(14) It was a long time since Nick had *looked* into a *stream* and *seen trout.*

Sentences (12) and (13) are examples of sentences containing no mention of the principal participant. Sentence (13) also shows zero cohesion with the preceding sentence and can be moved to several positions in the narrative (the sentence might be said to allow a restricted reordering). Sentence (12), *It was a hot day.,* shows zero cohesion with both the preceding and the following sentence and can be moved to almost any position in the passage studied; in other words sentence (12) is an example of a sentence that can range freely over the whole narrative (to be more precise, over the portion of the narrative under examination and some other portions not examined here). We might call (12) a free sentence, following Labov's and Waletzky's definition of a free clause.

To return to the scope of cohesive elements it may be added that the cohesive range of lexical items is usually larger than that of grammatical items. The only grammatical elements found to display a wide cohesive range are the third person pronouns and personal possessives signalling the participant involvement, and to a lesser extent the connector *however*. Other grammatical anaphoric elements appear to be restricted in cohesive function to adjacent sentences and clauses within sentences.

6.4. GRAMMATICAL FORMS IN VIEW OF COHESIVE FEATURES

In addition to the findings about the relationships obtaining between cohesion and style and between cohesion and discourse structure the present investigation has illuminated some aspects of grammatical structure. For example, the present study provides some insights into the functioning of connectors in English.

Certain connectors like *however* and *but*, which connect in the same way, differ in the scope of connection — *however* having a much larger scope than *but*. Some connectors like *however* can be moved to several positions in a sentence when indicating inter-sentence connection while others like *but* are restricted to one position — in the case of *but*, that at the beginning of the sentence. (See the description of the pair of James' sentences (22) — (23) in section 4.2. and the discussion of connectors in section 4.3.3. and in footnote 10 to Chapter 4.)

The study of cohesion has also shown that in a given text connectors are used to indicate relatedness of clauses much more frequently than that of sentences.

It appears from the present discussion of cohesion that connectors are usually placed before the second clause of the pair of adjacent clauses they join and thus these connectors can be seen as functioning anaphorically. Some connectors, however, can be placed at the beginning of the first clause in such a pair. In the latter case such connectors as *if* and *as* function cataphorically, as anticipatory signals of clause connection that is to follow. They seem to be restricted to subordinate clauses of circumstance or condition. The latter clauses will usually contain another cataphoric element. For example, in sentence (5) from the text by Hemingway, *As he watched them they changed their positions by quick angles, only to hold steady in the fast water again.*, the pronoun *them* of the clause introduced by the connector *as* is cataphoric in relation to *they* and *their* of the following clause.[9]

Still another group of connectors is formed by those that function in pairs, the first connector of the pair being cataphoric and the second anaphoric. An example of this group will be the pair of temporals *at first... then* functioning cohesively across the sentence boundary in Hemingway's sentences (9) and (10): *Nick did not see them at first. Then he saw them at the bottom of the pool, big trout looking to hold themselves on the gravel bottom in a varying mist of gravel and sand, raised in spurts by the current.*

We also note in connection with the above example that *them*, found in sentence (9) which contains the cataphoric temporal *at first*, functions cataphorically in relation to *them* and *the big trout* in sentence (10) which contains the anaphoric *then*. We can conclude therefore that the anaphoric or the cataphoric function of a connector is often paralleled by the same function of another cohesive element in the same clause or sentence and that cataphoric items in one sentence or clause may be matched by anaphoric items in the following sentence or clause, and vice versa.

[9] The most natural way to state that sentence out of context would be "As he watched them, the trout changed their positions...", which seems better than "As he watched the trout, they changed their positions...". In the first version *them* would clearly be cataphoric. But we recognize that the other interpretation is possible.

What has been said above about the function of connectors in the texts analyzed is a strong argument for studying cohesive elements as one integrated system of grammatical and lexical features, as the present investigation attempts to do. The usefulness of a descriptive framework such as the one presented in Chapter 3 is apparent.

Grammatical items whose function has been examined fall into two groups in respect of their anaphoric function: (1) those grammatical items, like the third person pronouns and personal possessives, that mark the involvement of the principal participant and (2) those that do not. Items from the first group can appear in the same anaphoric function (having the identical referent) in a large number of sentences, whether these sentences are adjacent or not, without the necessity of having their antecedents stated in the sentence immediately adjacent to the one in which they are found. Items from the second group on the other hand can be used only in the immediate neighborhood of either their antecedents or other anaphoric grammatical items referring to the same antecedents. A continuous line of anaphoric reference can be traced from one adjacent sentence to another in each case where items from the second group are used. Where this is impossible, as in the case of the demonstrative pronoun *this* in sentence (23) in James' text, the antecedent has to be restated in the sentence in which the anaphoric item appears. Conversely, when this continuous line of anaphoric reference stops this signals that the next occurrence of the same grammatical item may refer to a different antecedent (cf. the discussion of anaphora in section 4.3.2.). In other words we could say that to be cohesive, grammatical anaphoric items other than the third person pronouns and personal possessives referring to the principal participants require the presence of their antecedents, or other anaphoric elements referring to the same antecedent, in the immediately preceding sentence.

In the texts examined in this study zero anaphora was never found to function across sentence boundaries and the demonstrative pronouns *this* and *that* have been found to be least marked for their antecedents, and consequently the least definite in their anaphoric reference and hence least cohesive.

6.5. SUMMARY

In this study an attempt has been made to place cohesion in a theoretical framework of language organization. It has not been treated as a collection of unrelated grammatical categories but rather it has been shown to be a related and integrated part of the total structure of language. Thereafter a descriptive framework for the study of cohesion in written literary texts was set forth. The method of examining cohesion thus developed has been demonstrated in detail and the rationale for each decision has been explained.

This treatment opens new possibilities for linguistic studies of literary texts. Applied to the text by James the method of examining cohesion reveals a certain patterning of cohesive choices. The same technique applied to a text by Hemingway shows a quite different pattern. The application of the technique developed here to other literary texts may establish a relationship between a definite patterning of cohesive choices and a given literary style.

It has been demonstrated that the study of cohesion has implications for and can illuminate some problems of discourse structure, showing something about how the participant line, and to a lesser degree the event line, can be realized on the morphologic stratum. The study gives some insights about the ordering of sentences in such carefully structured discourse as written literary texts, as well as a few indications about the nature of units on the semologic stratum.

The study incidentally throws some light on a few problems of grammatical structure and composition. For example, the function of some grammatical forms such as connectors has been better understood because they are seen functioning in conjunction with other cohesive items.

Of course a great deal remains to be done. Not all the cohesive features that can be studied have been examined here. Elements omitted in the study (for example, sequence of tenses, modality, enation and agnation) could be included. Such an expanded framework would among other things reveal more about the organization of the event line. However, the limited framework as used in Chapters 4 and 5 seems sufficient for the study of those cohesive items which realize the participant line. It also demonstrates how the framework of cohesion may be used in the study of literary style.

APPENDIX I

TEXT OF THE FOURTH PARAGRAPH IN CHAPTER XLII
OF JAMES' *THE PORTRAIT OF A LADY*[1]

(1) Isabel's cheek burned when she asked herself if she had really
      married on a factitious theory, in order to do something
(2) finely appreciable with her money. But she was able to
      answer quickly enough that this was only half the story.
(3) It was because a certain ardour took possession of her —
      a sense of the earnestness of his affection and a delight in
(4) his personal qualities. He was better than any one else.
(5) This supreme conviction had filled her life for months, and
      enough of it still remained to prove to her that she could
(6) not have done otherwise. The finest — in the sense of being
      the subtlest — manly organism she had ever known had
      become her property, and the recognition of her having but
      to put out her hands and take it had been originally a sort
(7) of act of devotion. She had not been mistaken about the
      beauty of his mind; she knew that organ perfectly now.
(8) She had lived with it, she had lived *in* it almost — it appeared
(9) to have become her habitation. If she had been captured it
      had taken a firm hand to seize her; that reflection perhaps
(10) had some worth. A mind more ingenious, more pliant, more
      cultivated, more trained to admirable exercises, she had not
      encountered; and it was this exquisite instrument she had
(11) now to reckon with. She lost herself in infinite dismay when

[1] Henry James, *The Portrait of a Lady* (New York: Random House, The
Modern Library College Editions, 1966), 427-428. The numbers in the margin
mark the sentences which begin in corresponding lines. Reprinted by permission
of the publisher.

(12) she thought of the magnitude of *his* deception. It was a
wonder, perhaps, in view of this, that he didn't hate her

(13) more. She remembered perfectly the first sign he had given
of it — it had been like the bell that was to ring up the cur-

(14) tain upon the real drama of their life. He said to her one
day that she had too many ideas and that she must get rid of

(15) them. He had told her that already, before their marriage;
but then she had not noticed it: it had come back to her only

(16) afterwards. This time she might well have noticed it, because

(17) he had really meant it. The words had been nothing superficially, but when in the light of deepening experience she had

(18) looked into them they had then appeared portentous. He had
really meant it — he would have liked her to have nothing of

(19) her own but her pretty appearance. She had known she had
too many ideas; she had more even than he had supposed,
many more than she had expressed to him when he had asked

(20) her to marry him. Yes, she *had* been hypocritical; she had

(21) liked him so much. She had too many ideas for herself;
but that was just what one married for, to share them with

(22) some one else. One couldn't pluck them up by the roots,
though of course one might suppress them, be careful not

(23) to utter them. It had not been this, however, his objecting

(24) to her opinions; this had been nothing. She had no opinions — none that she would not have been eager to sacrifice

(25) in the satisfaction of feeling herself loved for it. What he had
meant had been the whole thing — her character, the way

(26) she felt, the way she judged. This was what she had kept in
reserve; this was what he had not known until he had found
himself — with the door closed behind, as it were — set

(27) down face to face with it. She had a certain way of looking

(28) at life which he took as a personal offence. Heaven knew that

(29) now at least it was a very humble, accommodating way! The
strange thing was that she should not have suspected from

(30) the first that his own had been so different. She had thought
it so large, so enlightened, so perfectly that of an honest man

(31) and a gentleman. Hadn't he assured her that he had no

superstitions, no dull limitations, no prejudices that had
(32) lost their freshness? Hadn't he all the appearance of a man
living in the open air of the world, indifferent to small
considerations, caring only for truth and knowledge and
believing that two intelligent people ought to look for them
together and, whether they found them or not, find at last
(33) some happiness in the search? He had told her he loved the
conventional; but there was a sense in which this seemed a
(34) noble declaration. In that sense, that of the love of harmony
and order and decency and of all the stately offices of life,
she went with him freely, and his warning had contained
(35) nothing ominous. But when, as the months had elapsed,
she had followed him further and he had led her into the
mansion of his own habitation, then, *then* she had seen where
she really was.

APPENDIX II

TEXT OF THE PASSAGE STUDIED FROM HEMINGWAY'S "BIG TWO-HEARTED RIVER": PART I.[1]

(1)   Nick looked at the burned-over stretch of hillside, where he had expected to find the scattered houses of the town and then walked down the railroad track to the bridge

(2), (3) over the river. The river was there. It swirled against

(4)   the log spiles of the bridge. Nick looked down into the clear, brown water, colored from the pebbly bottom, and watched the trout keeping themselves steady in the

(5)   current with wavering fins. As he watched them they changed their positions by quick angles, only to hold

(6)   steady in the fast water again. Nick watched them a long time.

(7)   He watched them holding themselves with their noses into the current, many trout in deep, fast moving water, slightly distorted as he watched far down through the glassy convex surface of the pool, its surface pushing and swelling smooth against the resistance of the log-driven

(8)   piles of the bridge. At the bottom of the pool were the

(9), (10) big trout. Nick did not see them at first. Then he saw them at the bottom of the pool, big trout looking to

[1] Ernest Hemingway, "Big Two-Hearted River: Part I", *The Short Stories of Ernest Hemingway* (New York: Charles Scribner's Sons, 1953), 209-211. The numbers in the margin mark the sentences which begin in corresponding lines. Reprinted by permission of Charles Scribner's Sons, New York; the Executors of the Ernest Hemingway Estate, and Jonathan Cape, Ltd., London.

hold themselves on the gravel bottom in a varying mist
of gravel and sand, raised in spurts by the current.

(11)   Nick looked down into the pool from the bridge.
(12), (13) It was a hot day. A kingfisher flew up the stream.
(14)   It was a long time since Nick had looked into a stream
(15), (16) and seen trout. They were very satisfactory. As the
shadow of the kingfisher moved up the stream, a big
trout shot upstream in a long angle, only his shadow
marking the angle, then lost his shadow as he came
through the surface of the water, caught the sun, and
then, as he went back into the stream under the surface,
his shadow seemed to float down the stream with the
current, unresisting, to his post under the bridge where
he tightened facing up into the current.

(17), (18)   Nick's heart tightened as the trout moved. He felt
all the old feeling.

(19), (20)   He turned and looked down the stream. It stretched
away, pebbly-bottomed with shallows and big boulders
and a deep pool as it curved away around the foot of a
bluff.

(21)   Nick walked back up the ties to where his pack lay
(22)   in the cinders beside the railway track. He was happy.
(23)   He adjusted the pack harness around the bundle, pulling
straps tight, slung the pack on his back, got his arms
through the shoulder straps and took some of the pull off
his shoulders by leaning his forehead against the wide
(24), (25) band of the tump-line. Still, it was too heavy. It was
(26)   much too heavy. He had his leather rod-case in his hand
and leaning forward to keep the weight of the pack high
on his shoulders he walked along the road that paralleled
the railway track, leaving the burned town behind in the
heat, and then turned off around a hill with a high, fire-

	scarred hill on either side onto a road that went back into
(27)	the country. He walked along the road feeling the ache
(28)	from the pull of the heavy pack. The road climbed steadi-
(29), (30)	ly. It was hard work walking up-hill. His muscles ached
(31)	and the day was hot, but Nick felt happy. He felt he had
	left everything behind, the need for thinking, the need
(32)	to write, other needs. It was all back of him.

(33)	From the time he had gotten down off the train and the
	baggage man had thrown his pack out of the open car
(34)	door things had been different. Seney was burned, the
	country was burned over and changed, but it did not
(35), (36)	matter. It could not all be burned. He knew that.
(37)	He hiked along the road, sweating in the sun, climbing
	to cross the range of hills that separated the railway from
	the pine plains.

(38)	The road ran on, dipping occasionally, but always
(39), (40)	climbing. Nick went on up. Finally the road after going
(41)	parallel to the burnt hillside reached the top. Nick
	leaned back against a stump and slipped out of the pack
(42)	harness. Ahead of him, as far as he could see, was the
(43)	pine plain. The burned country stopped off at the left
(44)	with the range of hills. On ahead islands of dark pine
(45)	trees rose out of the plain. Far off to the left was the line
(46)	of the river. Nick followed it with his eye and caught
	glints of the water in the sun.

(47)	There was nothing but the pine plain ahead of him,
	until the far blue hills that marked the Lake Superior
(48)	height of land. He could hardly see them, faint and far
(49)	away in the heat-light over the plain. If he looked too
(50)	steadily they were gone. But if he only half-looked they
	were there, the far-off hills of the height of land.

BIBLIOGRAPHY

Allen, Robert L.
  1961 "The Classification of English Substitute Words", *General Linguistics* 5, 7-20.
Ballard, D. Lee, Robert J. Conrad, and Robert E. Longacre
  1971 "The Deep and Surface Grammar of Interclausal Relations", *Foundations of Language* 7, 70-118.
Bloomfield, Leonard
  1933 *Language* (New York: Holt, Rinehart and Winston).
Bromley, H. Myron
  1972 "The Grammar of Lower Grand Valley Dani in Discourse Perspective", unpublished doctoral dissertation (Yale University).
Chafe, Wallace L.
  1970 *Meaning and the Structure of Language* (Chicago: University of Chicago Press).
Chatman, Seymour, and Samuel R. Levin, eds.
  1967 *Essays on the Language of Literature* (Boston: Houghton, Mifflin).
Chatman, Seymour, ed.
  1971 *Literary Style: A Symposium* (London and New York: Oxford University Press).
Cromack, Robert Earl
  1968 *Language Systems and Discourse Structure in Cashinawa* (= *Hartford Studies in Linguistics* 23) (Hartford, Connecticut: Hartford Seminary Foundation).
Crowell, Thomas H.
  1973 "Cohesion in Bororo Discourse", *Linguistics* 104, 15-27.
Crymes, Ruth
  1968 *Some Systems of Substitution Correlations in Modern American English* (The Hague: Mouton).
Daneš, František
  1969 "Zur Linguistische Analyse der Textstruktur", *Folia Linguistica* 4, 72-78.
Dressler, Wolfgang
  1969 "Modelle und Methoden der Textsyntax", *Folia Linguistica* 4, 64-71.
  1970 "Towards a Semantic Deep Structure of Discourse Grammar",

Papers from the Sixth Regional Meeting of the Chicago Linguistics Society (Chicago: University of Chicago, Department of Linguistics), 202-209.

Enkvist, Nils Erik, John Spencer, and Michael J. Gregory
1964   Linguistics and Style (London: Oxford University Press).

Fillmore, Charles J.
1968   "The Case for Case", Universals of Linguistic Theory, ed. by Emmon Bach and Robert T. Harms (New York: Holt, Rinehart & Winston), 1-88.
1970   "The Grammar of Hitting and Breaking", Readings in Transformational Grammar, ed. by Roderick A. Jacobs and Peter S. Rosenbaum (Waltham, Mass.: Ginn and Company), 120-133.

Fillmore, Charles, and D. Terence Langendoen, eds.
1971   Studies in Linguistic Semantics (New York: Holt, Rinehart & Winston).

Freeman, Donald C., ed.
1970   Linguistics and Literary Style (New York: Holt, Rinehart & Winston).

Garvin, Paul L., ed. and trans.
1964   A Prague School Reader on Esthetics, Literary Structure, and Style (Washington, D.C.: Georgetown University Press).

Gleason, H. A., Jr.
1964   "The Organization of Language: A Stratificational View", Monograph Series on Languages and Linguistics 17, ed. by C. I. J. M. Stuart (Washington, D.C.: Georgetown University Press), 75-96.
1965   Linguistics and English Grammar (New York: Holt, Rinehart & Winston).
1967   "Probings into No-Man's Land: The Marches of Linguistics, Semantics, Stylistics", unpublished lecture given at Bowdoin College, Conference on Linguistics and English Stylistics, May 4, 1967.
1968   "Contrastive Analysis in Discourse Structure", Monograph Series on Languages and Linguistics 21, ed. by James E. Alatis (= Monograph 21, Report of the 19th Annual Round Table Meeting) (Washington, D.C.: Georgetown University Press), 39-63.

Gleitman, Lila
1965   "Coordinating Conjunctions in English", Language 41, 260-293.

Greenbaum, Sidney
1969   Studies in English Adverbial Usage (London: Longmans).

Gregory, Michael
1966   "English Patterns: Perspectives for a Description of English", mimeographed preliminary version. (Later published at Toronto: Glendon College, York University, 1972.)

Grimes, Joseph, and Naomi Glock
1970   "A Saramaccan Narrative Pattern", Language 46, 408-425.

Gudschinsky, Sarah C.
1959   "Discourse Analysis of a Mazatec Text", International Journal of American Linguistics 15, 139-146.

Halliday, M. A. K.
1961   "Categories of the Theory of Grammar", Word 17, 241-292.
1962   "Descriptive Linguistics in Literary Studies", English Studies Today,

Third Series, ed. by G. I. Duthie (Edinburgh: University Press), 25-39 Reprinted in *Patterns of Language*, by Angus McIntosh and M. A. K. Halliday (London: Longmans, 1966), 56-59.

1964   "The Linguistic Study of Literary Texts", *Proceedings of the Ninth International Congress of Linguists*, ed. by Horace G. Lunt (The Hague: Mouton), 302-307. Reprinted in *Essays on the Language of Literature*, ed. by Seymour Chatman and Samuel R. Levin (Boston: Houghton, Mifflin Co.), 217-223.

1967   "Notes on Transitivity and Theme in English", *Journal of Linguistics* 3, 37-81, 199-244.

1969   "Options and Functions in the English Clause", *Brno Studies in English* 8, 81-88.

1970a "Language Structure and Language Function", *New Horizons in Linguistics*, ed. by John Lyons (Harmondsworth, Middlesex, England: Penguin Books), 140-165.

1970b "Functional Diversity in Language as Seen from a Consideration of Modality and Mood in English", *Foundations of Language* 6, 322-361.

1971   "Linguistic Function and Literary Style: An Inquiry into the Language of William Golding's *The Inheritors*", *Literary Style: A Symposium*, ed. by Seymour Chatman (London and New York: Oxford University Press), 330-365.

Halliday, Michael A. K., and Ruqaiya Hasan

1976   *Cohesion in Modern English* (Longmans English Language Series) (London, Longman).

Handscombe, Richard J.

1970   "George Herbert's 'The Collar': A Study in Frustration", *Language and Style* 3, 29-37.

Harris, Zellig S.

1946   "From Morpheme to Utterance", *Language* 22, 161-183.

1951   *Methods in Structural Linguistics* (Chicago: University of Chicago Press).

1952a "Discourse Analysis", *Language* 28, 1-30.

1952b "Discourse Analysis: A Sample Text", *Language* 28, 474-494.

1957   *Transformations and Discourse Analysis Papers* (Philadelphia: University of Pennsylvania), reissued in *Discourse Analysis Reprints* (= *Papers on Formal Linguistics* 2) (The Hague: Mouton, 1963).

1968   *Mathematical Structures of Language* (New York, John Wiley).

Harrison, Carl Howard

1970   "Syntactical Aspects of Asurini Monologue Discourse", unpublished doctoral dissertation (University of Pennsylvania).

Hartmann, R. R. K., and F. C. Stork

1972   *Dictionary of Language and Linguistics* (London: Applied Science Publishers).

Hasan, Ruqaiya

1964   "A Linguistic Study of Contrasting Features in the Style of Two Contemporary English Prose Writers", unpublished doctoral thesis (University of Edinburgh).

1967 "Linguistics and the Study of Literary Texts", *Études de Linguistique Appliquée* 5, 106-121.
1968 *Grammatical Cohesion in Spoken and Written English: Part One* (= *Programme in Linguistics and English Teaching*, Paper No. 7) (London: Longmans).
1971 "Rime and Reason in Literature", *Literary Style: A Symposium*, ed. by Seymour Chatman (London and New York: Oxford University Press), 299-326.

Hemingway, Ernest
1925 "Big Two-Hearted River: Part I", reprinted in *The Short Stories of Ernest Hemingway* (New York: Charles Scribner's Sons, 1953).
1940 *For Whom the Bell Tolls* (New York: Charles Scribner's Sons).

Hill, Archibald A.
1953 "A Sample Literary Analysis", *Monograph Series on Languages and Linguistics* 4, ed. by A. A. Hill (Washington, D.C.: Georgetown University Press), 87-93.
1959 *Introduction to Linguistic Structures* (New York: Harcourt, Brace and World).

Hjelmslev, Louis
1943 *Prolegomena to a Theory of Language*, transl. by F. J. Whitfield (Madison: University of Wisconsin Press, 1963).

Hockett, Charles F.
1939 "Potawatomi Syntax", *Language* 15, 235-248.
1958 *A Course in Modern Linguistics* (New York: Macmillan).
1968 *The State of the Art* (The Hague: Mouton).

Jacobs, Roderick A., and Peter S. Rosenbaum
1971 *Transformations, Style, and Meaning* (Waltham, Mass. and Toronto: Xerox College Publishing).

Jakobson, Roman
1960 "Closing Statement: Linguistics and Poetics", in *Style in Language*, ed. by Thomas Sebeok (Cambridge, Mass.: M.I.T. Press, 1964), 350-377.

James, Henry
1881 *The Portrait of a Lady* (New York: Random House, Modern Library College Editions, 1966).

Jolly, Grace
1970 "Nyisi Poetic Devices", unpublished doctoral dissertation (Hartford, Connecticut: Hartford Seminary Foundation).

Joos, Martin
1961 *The Five Clocks* (New York: Harcourt, Brace & World, 1967).

Katz, Jerrold J., and Jerry Fodor
1963 "The Structure of a Semantic Theory", *Language* 39, 170-210. Reprinted in *The Structure of Language: Readings in the Philosophy of Language* (Englewood Cliffs, N.J.: Prentice-Hall, 1964), 479-518.

Kipling, Rudyard
1902 *Just So Stories For Little Children* (Garden City, N.Y.: Doubleday, Page & Company, 1927).

Kittredge, Richard I.
1969 "Tense, Aspect, and Conjunction: Some Inter-Relation for English", unpublished doctoral dissertation (University of Pennsylvania).
Klammer, Thomas Paul
1971 "The Structure of Dialogue Paragraphs in Written English Dramatic and Narrative Discourse", unpublished doctoral dissertation (University of Michigan).
Koch, Walter A.
1965 "Preliminary Sketch of a Semantic Type of Discourse Analysis", *Linguistics* 12, 5-30.
1967 "A Linguistic Analysis of a Satire", *Linguistics* 33, 68-81.
Labov, William
1972 *Language in the Inner City: Studies in the Black English Vernacular* (Philadelphia: University of Pennsylvania Press).
Labov, William, and Joshua Waletsky
1967 "Narrative Analysis: Oral Versions of Personal Experience", *Essays on the Verbal Visual Arts (= Proceedings of the 1966 Annual Spring Meeting of the American Ethnological Society)*, ed. by June Helm (Seattle: University of Washington Press), 12-44.
Lakoff, Robin
1971 "If's, And's, and But's about Conjunction", *Studies in Linguistic Semantics*, ed. by Charles Fillmore and D. Terence Langendoen (New York: Holt, Rinehart & Winston), 115-149.
Lamb, Sydney M.
1966 *Outline of Stratificational Grammar* (Washington, D.C.: Georgetown University Press).
1970 "Linguistic and Cognitive Networks", *Cognition: A Multiple View*, ed. by Paul L. Garvin (New York: Spartan Books), 195-222.
1971 "The Crooked Path of Progress in Cognitive Linguistics", *Monograph Series on Languages and Linguistics* 24, ed. by Richard J. O'Brien, S.J. (Washington, D.C.: Georgetown University Press), 99-123.
Langendoen, D. Terence
1970 *Essentials of English Grammar* (New York: Holt, Rinehart & Winston).
Larson, Mildred L.
1965 "A Method for Checking Discourse Structure in Bible Translation", *Notes on Translation* 17, ed. by John Beekman (Glendale, Calif.: Summer Instituete of Linguistics).
Leech, Geoffrey N.
1965 "'This bread I break': Language and Interpretation", *Review of English Literature* 6.2, 66-75.
1969 *A Linguistic Guide to English Poetry* (London, Longman).
Levenston, E. A.
1972 "Narrative Technique in *Ulysses:* A Stylistic Comparison of 'Telemachus' and 'Eumaeus'", *Language and Style* 5, 260-275.
Lockwood, David G.
1972 *Introduction to Stratificational Linguistics* (New York: Harcourt Brace Jovanovich).

Longacre, Robert E.

1968 *Discourse, Paragraph, and Sentence Structure in Selected Philippine Languages*, Volumes I, II and III (Santa Ana, California: Summer Institute of Linguistics).

1970 "Sentence Structure as a Statement Calculus", *Language* 46, 783-815.

1972 *Hierarchy and Universality of Discourse Constituents in New Guinea Languages*, Volumes I and II (Washington, D.C.: Georgetown University Press).

Loos, Eugene

1963 "Copanahua Narrative Structure", *University of Texas Studies in Literature and Linguistics* 4, 699-742.

Loriot, James

1957 "Shipibo Discourse Analysis", *The Bible Translator*, July 1957 (New York: American Bible Society).

Loriot, James, and Barbara Hollenbach

1970 "Shipibo Paragraph Structure", *Foundations of Language* 6, 43-66.

McCrimmon, James M.

1967 *Writing with a Purpose*, 4th ed. (Boston: Houghton Mifflin), 109-130.

Moss, Leonard J.

1960 "Transitional Devices in Henry James", *CEA Critic* 22.2.

Nida, Eugene A.

1960 *A Synopsis of English Syntax*, ed. by Benjamin Elson (= *Linguistic Series* 4) (Norman, Oklahoma: Summer Institute of Linguistics, 1964).

1964 *Toward a Science of Translating* (Leyden: E. J. Brill).

Ohmann, Richard

1964 "Generative Grammars and the Concept of Literary Style", *Word* 20, 424-439. Reprinted in *Linguistics and Literary Style*, ed. by Donald C. Freeman (New York: Holt, Rinehart & Winston, 1970), 258-278.

Paton, Alan

1948 *Cry, the Beloved Country* (New York: Charles Scribner's Sons).

Pickett, Velma B.

1960 *The Grammatical Hierarchy of Isthmus Zapotec* (*Language Dissertation* 56) (Baltimore).

Pike, Kenneth L.

1964a "Discourse Analysis of Tagmemic Matrices", *Oceanic Linguistics* 3, 5-25.

1964b "Beyond the Sentence", *College Composition and Communication* 15, 129-135.

1967 *Language in Relation to a Unified Theory of the Structure of Human Behavior* (The Hague: Mouton).

Powlison, Paul S.

1965 "A Paragraph Analysis of a Yagua Folktale", *International Journal of American Linguistics* 31, 109-118.

Quirk, Randolph, Sidney Greenbaum, Geoffrey Leech, and Jan Svartvik

1972 *A Grammar of Contemporary English* (London: Longman).

Reich, Peter

1968 *Symbols, Relations, and Structural Complexity* (New Haven, Connecticut: Linguistic Automation Project, May 1968, Yale University).

1970a "Relational Networks", *Canadian Journal of Linguistics* 15, 95-110.
1970b "The English Auxiliaries: A Relational Network Description", *Canadian Journal of Linguistics* 16, 18-50.
Reid, Lawrence A.
1970 *Central Bontoc: Sentence, Paragraph and Discourse* (Norman, Oklahoma: Summer Institute of Linguistics).
Robins, R. H.
1964 *General Linguistics: An Introductory Survey* (London: Longmans, Green & Co.).
Ruhl, Charles
1973 "Prerequisites for a Linguistic Description of Coherence", *Language Sciences* 25, 15-18.
Ryle, G.
1954 *Dilemmas* (Cambridge: Cambridge University Press).
Sapir, Edward
1921 *Language* (New York: Harcourt, Brace and World, 1949).
Saussure, Ferdinand de
1915 *Course in General Linguistics*, trans. by Wade Baskin (New York: Philosophical Library, 1959).
Schnitzer, Marc L.
1971 "A Note on Tagmemic Discourse Analysis: Philosophical Argument", *Linguistics* 67, 72-82.
Scott, Charles T.
1965 *Persian and Arabic Riddles: A Language-Centered Approach to Genre Definition* (Supplement to *International Journal of American Linguistics*, Vol. XXXI, No. 4, part 2).
Scott, Sir Walter
1830 "Bonny Dundee", *Anthology of Romanticism*, 3rd ed., selected and edited by Ernest Bernbaum (New York: The Ronald Press, 1948), 448-449.
Sebeok, Thomas A., ed.
1960 *Style in Language* (Cambridge, Mass.: M.I.T. Press, 1964).
Sinclair, John McH.
1966 "Beginning the Study of Lexis", *In Memory of J. R. Firth*, ed. by C. Bazell, J. Catford, M. A. K. Halliday, and R. Robins (London: Longmans).
Smith, Carlota
1971 "Sentences in Discourse: An Analysis of a Discourse by Bertrand Russell", *Journal of Linguistics* 7, 213-235.
Southworth, F. C.
1967 "A Model of Semantic Structure", *Language* 43, 342-361.
Staal, J. F.
1968 "'And'", *Journal of Linguistics* 4, 79-81.
Stennes, Leslie H.
1969 *The Identification of Participants in Adamawa Fulani* (= *Hartford Studies in Linguistics* 24) (Hartford, Connecticut: The Hartford Seminary Foundation).

Stockwell, Robert P., Paul Schachter, and Barbara Hall Partee
 1973 *The Major Syntactic Structures of English* (New York: Holt, Rinehart
    & Winston).
Taber, Charles R.
 1966 *The Structure of Sango Narrative* (= *Hartford Studies in Linguistics*
    17) (Hartford, Connecticut: Hartford Seminary Foundation).
Thomas, Dylan
 1939 *The Collected Poems of Dylan Thomas* (New York: New Directions
    Books, 1953).
Waterhouse, Viola
 1963 "Independent and Dependent Sentences", *International Journal of
    American Linguistics* 29, 45-54.
Watson, Sheila
 1959 *The Double Hook* (= *New Canadian Library* 54) (Toronto: McClelland
    and Stewart Limited, 1969).
Watt, William W.
 1957 *An American Rhetoric*, revised edition (New York: Rinehart and Co.,
    1959).
Weinreich, Uriel
 1963 "On the Semantic Structure of Language", *Universals of Language*,
    ed. by Joseph H. Greenberg (Cambridge, Mass.: M.I.T. Press, 1966),
    142-216.
 1966 "Explorations in Semantic Theory", *Current Trends in Linguistics III*
    (The Hague: Mouton), 395-477.
Wheatley, James
 1973 "Pronouns and Nominal Elements in Bacairi Discourse", *Linguistics*
    104, 105-115.
Wheeler, Alva
 1967 "Grammatical Structure in Siona Discourse", *Lingua* 19, 60-77.
Williams, Joseph M.
 1966 "Some Grammatical Characteristics of Continuous Discourse", un-
    published doctoral dissertation (University of Wisconsin).
Winburne, John Newton
 1964 "Sentence Sequence in Discourse", *Proceedings of the Ninth Inter-
    national Congress of Linguists*, ed. by Horace G. Lunt (The Hague:
    Mouton), 1094-1098.
Winterowd, W. Ross
 1969 "The Grammar of Coherence", *College English* 31, 828-835.
Wise, Mary Ruth
 1968 "Identification of Participants in Discourse: A Study of Aspects of
    Form and Meaning in Nomatsiguenaga", unpublished doctoral
    dissertation (University of Michigan).

INDEX